HODDER SHP I[illegible]ONS

THE AMERICAN WEST

1840–95

ROBIN WICHARD

Hodder & Stoughton

A MEMBER OF THE HODDER HEADLINE GROUP

Robin Wichard is Head of History at the West Somerset Community College

ACKNOWLEDGEMENTS

To Carol, Joshua and Jack who have suffered so much in the creation of this book.

The author would like to thank Ms Pauline Butler for permission to use the revision questions at the end of this pack. The questions are based on an exercise which Ms Butler originally devised for use at the West Somerset Community College.

The publishers would like to thank the following for permission to reproduce material in this volume:
Thomas Nelson for an extract from *The American West* by Derek Wise (1984); Oxford University Press for the extract *from The Virginian* by Owen Wister; Time Life Publications for the extract from *The Soldiers* by D Nevin (1974); Reader's Digest for extracts from *The Story of the American West* (1977); Reed Consumer Books Limited for an extract from *American West* by R Hassrick (Octopus, 1975); Harper Collins Publishers for permission to use some illustrations and text that appeared in *The American West 1840–95* by Green (Collins Educational, 1977) and Heinemann Educational Publishers, a division of Reed Educational & Professional Publishing Ltd, for permission to use some illustrations and text that appeared in *The American West* by S Willoughby (1996) as a basis for some of the illustrations that appear in this publication.

The publishers would like to thank the following for permission to reproduce the following copyright photographs:
The Ronald Grant Archive: investigation 2.1 source C, issue 5 the big picture; The Salamander Picture Library: investigation 2.1 Blackfoot tepees, investigation 5.3 Jesse Chisholm; Exeter University Library: investigation 2.3 source G; investigation 2.5 courtesy of Frederic Remington Art Museum, Ogdensburg, NY; Peter Newark's Pictures: investigation 2.7 source C, investigation 5.3 Charles Goodnight, investigation 5.5 'The Last of 5,000', 'Riding the Line of the Wire Fence', investigation 6.1 an illustration showing 'Large amounts of surplus land...', investigation 6.4 a poster for barbed wire, an illustration showing a wind pump, issue 8 an illustration showing 'A steam engine of the Central Pacific Railroad...', investigation 9.1 source B; Black American West Museum and Heritage Center, Denver, USA: investigation 5.1 source A; investigation 5.1 source F courtesy of The Witte Museum, San Antonio, Texas; Montana Historical Society: investigation 5.2; Austin History Center, Austin Public Library, photo ID#PICA 08674: investigation 5.3; Dickinson County Historical Society: investigation 5.3 Joseph McCoy; John Atkins: investigation 5.6 'Wyoming Wildbunch'; The Denver Public Library, Western History Collection: investigation 5.6 an advertisement for 'Tomkins' Real Wild West'; Kansas State Historical Society: investigation 6.1 'Droughty' Kansas, investigation 6.3, investigation 9.1 source A, source B, source E, source F, source H; Nebraska State Historical Society: investigation 6.1 an illustration showing a Nebraska couple, investigation 6.2 an illustration showing a Nebraska soddie; Western History Collections, University of Oklahoma: issue 7 an illustration showing Cattle Annie and Little Britches, issue 9 an illustration showing Judge Roy Bean; Mary Evans Picture Library: investigation 4.1 an illustration showing the murder of Joseph Smith, investigation 4.3 source B, investigation 6.4 an illustration showing how 'Machinery greatly eased the pressure...', investigation 8.1; investigation 10.2 an illustration showing buffalo skulls courtesy of Burton Historical Collection of the Detroit Public Library; Seaver Center for Western History Research, Los Angeles County Museum of Natural History: investigation 10.3; V&A Picture Library: investigation 11.1 source A; US National Archives and Records Administration: investigation 11.1 source I; Robin Wichard: investigation 6.2 'a family in their Sunday best', investigation 13.2; *The Rocky Mountains* by TBH Stenhome (1874): investigation 4.1 (except for the illustration showing the murder of Joseph Smith); The Smithsonian Institute: investigation 2.6.

Every effort has been made to trace and acknowledge ownership of copyright. The publishers will be glad to make suitable arrangements with any copyright owners whom it has not been possible to contact.

Orders: please contact Bookpoint Ltd, 39 Milton Park, Abingdon, Oxon OX14 4TD. Telephone: (44) 01235 400414, Fax: (44) 01235 400454. Lines are open from 9.00–6.00, Monday to Saturday, with a 24 hour message answering service. Email address: orders@bookpoint.co.uk

British Library Cataloguing in Publication Data
A catalogue record for this title is available from The British Library

ISBN 0 340 70487 X

First published 1998
Impression number 10 9 8 7 6 5 4 3 2 1
Year 2004 2003 2002 2001 2000 1999 1998

Cover photos: main picture – 'Evening on Crow Reservation, Montana' (oil on canvas), Private Collection, reproduced courtesy of The Bridgeman Art Library, London; inset picture – 'Black cowboy, James Arthur Walker', reproduced courtesy of the Black American West Museum and Heritage Center, Denver, USA.

Illustrations by Tom Cross and Chris Brown.
Typeset by Wearset, Boldon, Tyne and Wear.
Printed in Great Britain for Hodder & Stoughton Educational, a division of Hodder Headline Plc, 338 Euston Road, London NW1 3BH by Hobbs the Printers, Totton, Hants.

Contents

Teacher's notes

This pack of materials was born out of the need to address the difficulty many students have with the volume of knowledge and understanding required at GCSE.

Somehow there often appears to be a gulf between the quality of teaching and the quality of learning. The pressure of league tables and performance indicators have demanded a review of current practice.

A number of generalisations can be made:

- Much teaching assumes that the students are as familiar with the syllabus as the staff teaching it. Lesson recaps are generally used to place new work in the context of that immediately preceding it but not necessarily in the context of the module as a whole.
- Teachers might feel that because there is so much material in the available textbooks there is an obligation to teach it all, whereas it is arguably better for many students to learn less but with a greater understanding.
- There is a tendency to measure educational value by the volume of work evident in a student's exercise book or folder. With the emphasis on extended writing there is pressure to ensure that such exercises are set despite the fact that some students cannot easily cope with the task and have not necessarily understood the work unless appropriate preparation has been undertaken.

Hence these materials.

This is *not* a textbook. This pack does not pretend to be exhaustive in content, merely to raise some of the key issues and provide an opportunity to study the subject through structured tasks.

As such, it can be used in a number of ways:

- As a basis for teaching the American West alongside the established textbooks.
- Additional resources used as extension materials to promote enquiry.
- As a means of reinforcing specific areas of the course by providing end of topic assessment exercises.
- By using the context pages as a revision guide and the exercises as revision tasks.
- As a bank of materials available at short notice to provide set work in the event of staff absence.

Structure

At the front of the pack there is a single page entitled the **big picture**. This is an attempt to synthesise the whole module and present it in a format that the students can access. This will enable them to place any work they undertake into context and can be used by teachers to provide coherence to the teaching package.

Issues

The pack is divided into a series of key **issues**. These can be equated with the main sections of the syllabus and the main chapters of most textbooks. Each issue is prefaced by a **big picture** page which offers a context for the investigations which follow and contains selected, key information which can be used in the subsequent **investigations**.

Investigations

Within each issue there are one or more **investigations** which focus on a specific question. The investigation will contain a further body of relevant information which will allow all students access to the **tasks** which follow. Where appropriate, students can then be directed to the relevant sections of textbooks for additional, independent research.

• Tasks

Within each investigation there are a number of graded **tasks**. In response to either sources or key information students will be asked initially to reformat or synthesise the information through card exercises, charts, diagrams, source interpretation etc. Where the task focus is deemed to warrant it, an additional task may be set to further develop familiarity and understanding of the material. The final task will generally solicit a piece of extended writing in response to the original question posed by the investigation. The phrasing of this final task is designed to encourage independent research and echo the phraseology of the GCSE examinations (which require students to use the material provided *and* their own knowledge). In a number of cases **writing frames** have been provided to structure student responses.

To reinforce understanding, where appropriate, tasks are linked by reference to others on a similar theme – for example **investigation 3.1** (Why did people move onto the Plains?) can be linked to **investigation 4.1** (Why did the Mormons move to the Great Salt Lake?) and **investigation 6.1** (Who were the homesteaders and why did they come to the Plains?).

This pattern of revisiting elements in the pack is an effective way of reinforcing learning *and* understanding of the subject.

Issues and investigations

Issue 1: The Great Plains

Aim: to familiarise students with the harsh and unique environment of the Great Plains and provide a context for understanding why Indians lived the way they did.

A map showing the geographical regions of the US is shown in the 'big picture'. Preparatory work could include more detailed research into the precise geographical location of the Plains and the natural features that border it (rivers, mountains etc.).

Investigation 1.1 What were the Plains like?

This investigation aims to provide some understanding of the Plains through sources. Unlike many textbooks the sources do not include references to changes made to the Plains as a result of White settlement as this will emerge in later work.

- **Task 1:** This exercise involves source interpretation and evaluation. Students are asked to read and question the information provided. The different views expressed by Whites and Indians will provide a vehicle into the next issue.
- **Task 2:** This task requires students to select evidence from the earlier tasks in order to produce a piece of extended writing.
- **Task 3:** Aims to build on the information obtained from task 1 by re-sorting key issues into positive and negative comments. The point could be made that a comment can be positive or negative depending on your viewpoint – Indian or White – hence reinforcing the messages from task 1. Students uncomfortable with source work at this stage of the course may wish to start at task 2 and leave out task 1.

Issue 2: The Plains Indians and their environment

Aim: to recognise the number and diversity of Plains Indian peoples and the way in which they adapted to their environment.

The 'big picture' deals with the major Indian groups and their origins, and it loosely sets the scene for the clash of cultures which will emerge later.

Investigation 2.1 How did the Indians adapt to life on the Plains?

Through a study of the Indian tepee many other aspects of the Indian life can be accessed – for example the dependence on the buffalo, nomadism etc.

- **Task 1:** Unusually, this first task is a piece of extended writing *but* supported by a writing frame with clear prompts. Teachers may prefer to substitute a different exercise requiring less writing but achieving the same goals – for example a spider diagram. Such an exercise may then lead students into task 1.
- **Task 2:** This exercise uses sources to consider different views of the Indian tepee. Students should already have a good working knowledge of the tepee and how well it was designed and so should be able to recognise bias etc. in the sources.

Investigation 2.2 How did the Indians use the Plains?

All textbooks deal admirably with the Indians' dependence on the buffalo but few actually stress the use made of plants in Indian society. The material presented here comes from unpublished research on Southern Plains Indians undertaken at the University of New Mexico. This represents a very small number of plants and their uses but serves to illustrate the point.

- **Task 1:** After looking at the diagram students are asked to categorise the information about plants into areas of use. This will serve to reinforce the students' understanding of the diversity of plant use.
- **Task 2:** This is a piece of extended writing. By extracting information from a quote (which is provided in full later in **investigation 2.3**) students have a very clear proposition to which to respond and the information from task 1 will offer a possible structure – each area of plant use could form the basis of a paragraph or sentence.

Investigation 2.3 What were the Indians' attitudes towards the land?

Having studied the way in which the environment served to shape the Indians' lifestyle in the two previous investigations, students should now have a clear context for understanding why the earth was sacred to the Indians.

- **Task 1:** The Indians themselves are best able to express their own views on the earth. A conflicting White view is offered as a means of beginning to emphasise the cultural differences between the two peoples.
- **Task 2:** This exercise involves extended writing through empathy. This is still a very useful way of encouraging students to articulate the thought of other cultures – especially when they have the knowledge needed to do it well.

Investigation 2.4 How did the Indians use the buffalo?

To emphasise the Indians' dependence on the buffalo and the vast amount of resources that can be obtained from a buffalo.

- **Task 1:** This exercise simply requires the patience to extract the information from the sources and enter it onto a chart. This will then give some idea of the amount of buffalo parts that can be used. The diagram beneath is intended to aid those less anatomically inclined.

- **Task 2:** Having recognised the range of parts that can be used there is a need to consider the uses to which they can be put. This is essential if students are really to understand the extent to which the Indians depended on the buffalo.

- **Task 3:** This task attempts to introduce the destruction of the buffalo as a means of considering Indian dependence. It requires rather more thought than simply responding to the original question and may benefit from some preparatory work, such as class discussion.

Investigation 2.5 What were the Indians' attitudes towards war and bravery?

An attempt to introduce Indian values and encourage comparison with those of White society (another example of preparing for the 'clash of culture' work to follow). It also helps to explain the feathered bonnets with which westerns are so enamoured and helps to show that they were not the symbols of leadership as so many assume.

- **Task 1:** Again empathy is used as a vehicle for considering Indian attitudes. Colonel Dodge's views are used to promote a response. A writing frame is provided to structure student responses and avoid irrelevance.

Investigation 2.6 The role of women and children in Indian society

All too often the study of the Plains Indians focuses on the role of men and tends to suggest – albeit indirectly – that women played a very small supporting role. This exercise attempts to reverse that image and also to introduce the role of children. The investigation can be used in conjunction with investigation 6.3 and investigation 7.1 which consider the role of White women on the Plains.

- **Task 1:** A relatively simple interpretation exercise listing the tasks undertaken by women and a follow-up exercise which asks pupils to explain how those tasks gave women power.

- **Task 2:** Again, a relatively simple explanation of what Indian education consisted of and why.

- **Task 3:** A consolidation exercise involving extended writing using a writing frame to enable pupils to structure a response to a given proposition.

Investigation 2.7 The Indian: noble Indian or savage barbarian?

This exercise aims to encourage students to justify views of the Indians and begin to recognise how those views have come about.

- **Task 1:** This exercise requires the sources to be classified into those *for* and those *against* the Indians.

- **Task 2:** This builds on task 1 by beginning to look at where the different types of source come from. The pattern that should emerge is that the further removed the author was from the Indians (and therefore the more ignorant of the Indian culture) the more negative was the view expressed. This can perhaps best be achieved by class discussion but if the exercise is to be used by supply/cover staff then a written outcome might be preferable.

- **Task 3:** Assuming that the anticipated patterns have emerged from the source analysis then task 3 presents a proposition to which the students should be able to respond positively.

Issue 3: The reasons for White settlement on the Plains

Aim: to understand the diversity of motives behind White settlement on the Plains and the reasons used to justify it – such as **manifest destiny**.

Investigation 3.1 Why did people move onto the Plains?

An attempt to consider some of the most common reasons for White settlement on the Plains and introduce the ideas of push and pull factors in determining movement.

- **Task 1:** A straightforward exercise which requires students to decide for themselves whether given reasons are push or pull factors.

- **Task 2:** A consolidation exercise in the form of a piece of extended writing. The information gathered from the 'big picture' and task 1 should make this relatively easy.

Issue 4: The Mormons and Salt Lake City

Aim: to recognise the very specific reasons for Mormon movement onto the Plains and the importance of Brigham Young in the successful completion of the task.

Investigation 4.1 Why did the Mormons move to the Great Salt Lake?

This investigation builds on investigation 3.1 by focusing in depth on one group of settlers and their motivation.

● **Task 1:** This is a sorting exercise which introduces students to the terms **political**, **social**, **religious** and **economic** by encouraging them to sort the various reasons for Mormon movement into these categories.

● **Task 2:** This builds on task 1 by focusing on the actions of the Gentiles against the Mormons in response to the hatred studied in the previous task.

● **Task 3:** This is an extended writing exercise which builds on information gathered in the previous two tasks. Although no structured writing frame has been provided for this work one could be conceived or, alternatively, the students themselves could generate one from brainstorming key ideas.

Investigation 4.2 How important was Brigham Young to the Mormons?

No one at the time thought that the Mormons would be successful in their new home. That they were is undoubtedly due in large part to Brigham Young. This exercise focuses on Young's role in the move to the Great Salt Lake.

● **Task 1:** Sources are used as a way into identifying the problems faced by the Mormons and Young's role in overcoming them. The exercise requires students to identify the problems and what solutions were offered.

● **Task 2:** Armed with a list of problems and their solutions, students will be in a fairly strong position to use that information in order to assess Young's importance. Extra reinforcement can be given by a class discussion prior to starting task 2. This discussion could flag up key phrases and ideas, for example, students could be asked to volunteer examples to go under the headings **important** and **not important**. This could then act as a frame for writing the final product.

Investigation 4.3 What was the Great Salt Lake like?

A source-based exercise which aims to use contradictory views of the Salt Lake to reinforce the power Young had in overcoming negative views.

● **Task 1:** This task focuses attention on the advantages and disadvantages of the Great Salt Lake through source interpretation and evaluation.

Investigation 4.4 How well did the Mormons cope at the Great Salt Lake?

A brief summary of the Mormons at Salt Lake City and their changing relations with the US Government.

● **Task 1:** This exercise focuses on the changes made by the Mormons to the area around the Salt Lake.

● **Task 2:** This exercise encourages an understanding of chronology and the sequence of events which led to the formation of the state of Utah in 1890. The results are tabulated in the form of a flow diagram but a timeline could be used instead.

Issue 5: The cowboys and cattle

Aim: to explain the truth about the cowboys and their role and to examine why the popular image of cowboys as gunslinging heroes has emerged.

Investigation 5.1 Who were the cowboys?

When did you last see a black cowboy in a western (apart from the scene with baked beans in *Blazing Saddles*)? Using sources this task attempts to identify some of the characteristics of the true cowboys.

● **Task 1:** The source interpretation and evaluation here is geared to building up an accurate picture of the cowboys while reinforcing source skills.

● **Task 2:** This task builds on the information gathered from the sources in order to answer the original question.

Investigation 5.2 What did the cowboys wear and why?

Again, an attempt to dispel the popular image by focusing on primary sources and logic – when it is pointed out, few students cannot see that firing a gun near cattle is not advisable!

● **Task 1:** This exercise generally appeals to all students. The cowboy in the picture is actually showing the size of noose needed to rope a cow.

Investigation 5.3 Why did the Long Drives begin and who was responsible?

To understand the origins of the Long Drives, it is necessary to understand the impact that the American Civil War had on the nation. Most textbooks give the event a line or two and this pack does only marginally more, due to pressure of space. The legacy of Mexican cattle ranching is also considered in the background information provided. The section dealing with the events leading to a Long Drive could be used as the basis for work on the jobs undertaken by a cowboy – perhaps a spider diagram identifying the different jobs.

● **Task 1:** A causation exercise which uses a flow diagram to explain the events, in sequence, leading to the Long Drives. Students may want to do a rough draft before committing themselves finally to paper.

● **Task 2:** Building on the information gathered in task 1, this exercise asks the students to consider the importance of the Civil War as opposed to other factors in starting the Long Drives. Clearly, without the War there would have been no Long Drives but there is still a need to consider other influences – such as the role of Joseph McCoy and Charles Goodnight. A brainstorming session might provide other influences for the students to consider.

Investigation 5.4 What was life like for cowboys on the Long Drive?

Having explained to students through earlier work that the cowboys did not spend most of their time either battling Indians or engaging in blazing gun battles, there is a need to consider what they actually did. In reality, the boring monotony of much of it explains why there are very few movies based on the Long Drive (just one, to be precise). This is attempted through the medium of a game involving cards. The game board will need to be assembled in advance and the cards copied and cut out.

- **Task 1:** The task here is to play the game. It is rigged to ensure that all players will have opportunities to discover the real monotony of the job by repeating the cards with the typical events on them.

- **Task 2:** This task runs concurrently with task 1. As the game is played, players will need to keep a record of what happens to them. This will be recorded in the form of a journal.

- **Task 3:** Using the information gathered from the game, students should be able to assemble the information into a logical piece of extended writing. If necessary, the teacher can solicit information from the class before the writing starts, in the form of a debrief – 'what did you find that you spent most of your time doing'? etc. The findings can then be written on the board to serve as a writing frame.

Investigation 5.5 How and why did cattle ranching change by 1890?

This exercise looks at the end of the open range and at the impact that it had on the cowboy. This leads into the next task which will consider why a job lasting less than 20 years has had such an impact on the image of the American West.

- **Task 1:** Given that the information for this exercise is already clearly laid out, the task asks students to consider which of the causes shown is likely to have had the greatest impact – and why. Again, a class brainstorm can serve to gain ideas.

- **Task 2:** The famous Russell sketch, *Last of the 5,000*, is used as a prompt to ask why such events happened. Students have the main causes on a diagram and will also have had the opportunity to consider the relative importance of each factor.

- **Task 3:** The picture of the cowboy is a clue as to the changes that the end of the open range had on the cowboy. Using the information from the task students should be able to consider other changes too. In addition to considering what the cowboys were forced to do, they should also think about what they could not now do and why.

Investigation 5.6 Why are the images of the cowboys often so far from reality?

Having established that the popular image of the cowboy is inaccurate, this exercise considers how the image has come about. It can also be linked with investigation 2.7 (The Indian: noble Indian or savage barbarian?) as a way of showing how bias and inaccuracy can evolve.

- **Task 1:** This exercise is simply asking students to produce a list of the various reasons why the myth has come about from the information provided.

- **Task 2:** Although not leading directly to a written outcome there is no real reason why it should not if appropriate. The exercise attempts to consider which of the reasons studied in task 1 has had the biggest impact on the growth of the myth.

Issue 6: The homesteaders

Aim: to identify the diverse groups of people who came to the Plains to farm and the experience they had.

Investigation 6.1 Who were the homesteaders and why did they come to the Plains?

This work leads on from investigations 3.1 and 4.1 and helps to build up a detailed picture of the western settlers. The homesteaders were the first people to attempt to change the Plains and this work needs to be undertaken in that context.

- **Task 1:** The information needed to answer this task is so clearly laid out – the 'big picture' information is almost a writing frame by itself!

- **Task 2:** This exercise, requires students to consider the relative importance of the different factors. Here the question is framed around a proposition and, in order to gain the most marks, students will need to consider all reasons in order to reach a decision.

Investigation 6.2 How did the homesteaders survive on the Plains?

Using sources and a sectional diagram students are asked to look in detail at the soddie. Some exam papers have tended to portray the soddie as a hovel (and many were) but there were two-storey soddies with proper tile roofs and were in use long after they could have been replaced with timber structures.

● **Task 1:** A simple advantages and disadvantages exercise based on the sources provided. This task will provide a body of knowledge which can be used as the frame for answering task 2.

● **Task 2:** A piece of extended writing born out of task 1. Rather than simply asking 'what were the advantages and disadvantages of the soddies?' the question deliberately concentrates attention on their merits.

Investigation 6.3 What was life like for women on the Plains?

This investigation links well with issue 7 and investigation 7.1 (How important were women on the Plains?). Because most students find it easier to empathise with an individual, 'The Story of Sarah Sim' is included as an example.

● **Task 1:** A re-sorting exercise which requires students to identify the problems faced by the women and the way in which they attempted to deal with them. Conclusions can be recorded on the chart provided.

● **Task 2:** A summary of findings from task 1 and 'the big picture' in the form of a piece of extended writing.

Investigation 6.4 What problems did the homesteaders face and how did they deal with them?

● **Task 1:** Using the cards, students try to match problem cards with solutions. Students will soon see that some problems can be overcome but, given the harsh climate of the Plains, some cannot. The figures for homestead repossessions in Kansas serve to illustrate the failure rate.

● **Task 2:** An extended writing exercise building on information gathered in task 1.

Issue 7: The role of women on the Plains

Aim: a study of the achievements of women on the Plains which links with investigation 6.3 (What was life like for women on the Plains?) but goes on to consider women in towns as well. The west provided many opportunities for women which were not available in the east – and they took them!

Investigation 7.1 How important were women on the Plains?

An attempt to give women on the Plains, and their achievements, the credit they deserve. Few textbooks actually acknowledge women beyond homesteaders; hence the value of this exercise. It also serves to show that the west was not entirely a frontier devoid of culture.

● **Task 1:** A re-sorting exercise using a spider diagram to record collected data.

● **Task 2:** A loaded question, but one which certainly encourages students to think about the contribution that women made. They should be encouraged to consider the experiences of homesteaders (investigation 6.3) when working through this task.

Issue 8: The impact of the railroads on the Plains

Aim: the railroads are often cited as an important factor in encouraging settlement but students are rarely given an opportunity to consider how that was achieved.

Investigation 8.1 What impact did the railroads have on the settlement of the Plains?

The railroads may have benefited the White settlers but Indians would never extol their virtues.

● **Task 1:** A series of positive and negative statements about the railroads have been jumbled up. These need to be sorted and placed onto appropriate spider diagrams.

● **Task 2:** The findings from task 1 are studied. It should become apparent that the Indians suffered as much as the settlers benefited. This task can be accomplished through class discussion.

● **Task 3:** A piece of extended writing based on the findings of the two previous tasks.

Issue 9: Government, law and order on the Plains

Aim: although there were clear difficulties establishing law and order in the far flung territories, the vast majority of the population were law abiding, as this exercise aims to show.

Investigation 9.1 How wild was the west?

The emphasis here is on sources which stress the success of law and order rather than on those who violated the law.

● **Task 1:** A chart is used to show the different elements of law and order in the west.

● **Task 2:** Another loaded proposition designed to reverse the popular image of the west as a totally lawless environment. As with all other extended writing exercises, a frame or class discussion can be used to guide students.

Investigation 9.2 How important was the US Government in the settlement of the Plains?

This investigation builds on from investigation 9.1 which concentrated on law and order. A spider diagram summarises the other contributions made by the Government. Other factors which encouraged settlement are also considered.

- **Task 1:** A piece of extended writing based on a consideration of the relative importance of the Government's efforts.

Issue 10: The US Government and the Indian problem

Aim: to explain clearly the various phases of Government policy and the reasons for their failure.

Investigation 10.1 Why were Indian and White lifestyles always leading to conflict?

An exercise which builds on work covered in issue 3 (The reasons for White settlement on the Plains). A number of key points are placed on two spider diagrams to aid comparison. The list is far from exhaustive and class discussion can be effectively used to suggest other points which can be added to the diagrams.

- **Task 1:** A re-sorting exercise which encourages direct comparison of White and Indian views.

- **Task 2:** A piece of extended writing utilising information gleaned from the previous task and other work.

Investigation 10.2 How did the US Government attempt to deal with the Indian problem?

An attempt has been made to divide US Government policy into four clearly identified phases. The problem here has always been the sheer volume of information which the students need to learn. Here the emphasis has been to minimise the content and explain the reasons for failure clearly.

- **Task 1:** The aim of the exercise is for students to synthesise the key points of each policy and the major reasons for failure, recording the information on a chart. The act of recording the information will require them to read the material provided and attempt to determine the major points.

- **Task 2:** To reinforce understanding of the sequence of events a timeline is proposed which will stand alongside the chart in task 1 as a means of recording the major points.

- **Task 3:** Understanding of the material can then be assessed through the consolidation exercise – a piece of extended writing. The chart from task 1 and the timeline from task 2 will serve as writing frames, as will the names given to each major phase of policy.

Investigation 10.3 Sand Creek: victory or massacre?

The events of Sand Creek have been recorded as major contributing factors to the later Indian conflicts (especially Red Cloud's War). What actually happened is still unclear although the evidence from the various inquiries does give a fairly good impression that certain key characters were not telling the whole truth. The testimony of individuals at the inquiries has formed the basis of this exercise.

- **Task 1:** Using the wording of the investigation title as a guide, students are asked to attempt to sort the clue cards into those supporting the idea of a justified victory and those which suggest a massacre. Clearly some guidance will be needed as to how to determine which is which. It might be best if the students themselves were able to determine the criteria to be used which could then be written up for all to use. There is no right or wrong answer – it is a subjective exercise.

- **Task 2:** The key issues to emerge are whether or not there were scalps, and whether or not the Indian dead were mutilated. There are other questions which could also be asked such as 'How many Indians were killed?'. Students are encouraged to attempt to answer these questions and consider the reasons for the conflicting evidence. While undertaking these tasks the students will be learning about the events at Sand Creek.

Issue 11: The Plains wars: Custer and the Little Bighorn

Aim: to consider the complexity of Custer's character and to use that information to attempt an explanation of what happened at the Little Bighorn. Although this work does not solicit it, there is no reason why an additional question could not be added asking students to evaluate Custer's personal role in the defeat. Recent archaeological evidence is used to explain the sequence of events during the battle.

Investigation 11.1 Who was the real Custer?

Custer has become a legend in American history but not everyone at the time believed that he deserved the reputation for outstanding bravery and courage that he has since acquired.

- **Task 1:** A series of sources are presented reflecting both positive and negative views of the General. Students are asked to read the sources and determine which comments are positive and so on, recording the findings on a chart.

- **Task 2:** A piece of extended writing based on the findings from task 1.

● **Task 3:** Having considered the different views of Custer, this exercise asks students to consider what sort of person he was. A brainstorming of possible adjectives might help to provide a structure. Any adjectives used (e.g. brave etc.) will need to be supported by reference to the sources.

Investigation 11.2 Why was Custer defeated?

Here cards are used as a focus for the enquiry.

● **Task 1:** The cards are used to determine short-term and long-term causation.

● **Task 2:** The cards are used to consider personal and impersonal causation.

● **Task 3:** The findings of tasks 1 and 2 are pulled together in a chart which requires students to make judgements, based on the evidence, about the relative strengths and weaknesses of the two sides. If this is done effectively it should soon become apparent that Custer was defeated because all of the contributing factors were against him.

● **Task 4:** If task 3 is successful then it will provide a frame for writing the answer to this task.

Issue 12: The defeat of the Plains Indians

Aim: to review events after the Battle of the Little Bighorn and recognise the impact that Custer's death had on the American people. Also to become familiar with the fate of various important individuals/groups.

Investigation 12.1 How were the Indians defeated?

A relatively brief introduction to a very broad topic.

● **Task 1:** A straightforward exercise designed to gather information and present it in a clear and accessible format.

● **Task 2:** A timeline exercise. There is a lot to cover here and a timeline is a useful way of organising the material in a way that is clear and accessible.

● **Task 3:** An attempt to empathise with the US Government by attempting to consider the Ghost Dance religion from their perspective. Such an approach may not be fashionable, but it is valid and leads away from stereotyping the Government's actions as mindlessly cruel and aggressive.

Issue 13: How successful was the US Government in the destruction of the Indians?

Aim: Having recognised the various measures taken to solve 'the Indian problem', it seems appropriate that a few pages be given over to an assessment of the success of such measures and the status of the American Indian in contemporary American society.

Investigation 13.1 Why did the US Government try to destroy the Indians?

An attempt to place the action taken against the Indians in the context of White beliefs in manifest destiny – hence the links back to issue 3 (The reasons for White settlement on the Plains). It is important that students see the actions of the Government in context if they are to truly understand the purpose of such actions.

● **Task 1:** A useful consolidation exercise which attempts to demonstrate understanding of the Government's actions by offering explanations/ justifications for the various measures taken. This aims to ensure that the student recognises both sides of the issue. There is no doubt that the US Government did need to take some action to address the problems of overcrowding etc. in the east.

● **Task 2:** Using a clear quotation from the American Declaration on Independence, this exercise encourages students to make a judgement on the actions of the US Government.

Investigation 13.2 How do Indians live today?

A short attempt to bring the story up to date by considering the role of the Indian in contemporary American society.

● **Task 1:** Using a few examples to illustrate the ways in which Indians have managed to preserve their traditions and, at the same time, to adapt to the demands of contemporary American society, this task encourages students to see the American Indian as a living entity and not merely a character relegated to the pages of a history book.

Revision questions and the American West timeline

The revision questions are intended to act as self-testing prompts, although they could easily be adapted for more formal assessment of knowledge and understanding. The questions all require relatively short answers and are grouped in broad themes rather than by issue and investigation. The answers should be contained within the body of the text but clearly any additional knowledge will be of benefit. The timeline provides a chronology of the main events which occurred immediately before and during the years 1840 to 1895.

THE BIG PICTURE

THE GREAT PLAINS

Any study of the Plains is really a study of how different groups of people **saw, used** and **changed** the Plains and how these different views led to conflict.

THE INDIANS (Native Americans)

Their relationship with the Plains and views on land ownership (dependent on the Plains).

Indian culture and lifestyle; beliefs and traditions.

Noble Indian or savage barbarian?

Indian attempts to deal with the spread of White settlement onto the Plains.

THE WHITES

The different views of the Whites.

MORMONS AND MINERS (crossing the Plains)

COWBOYS AND CATTLEMEN (using the Plains)

HOMESTEADERS (changing the Plains)

GOVERNMENT, LAW AND ORDER (civilising the Great Plains)

CONFLICT

INDIANS AND WHITES: A clash of cultures

US GOVERNMENT POLICIES

Sand Creek massacre ← **THE INDIAN WARS** → The Little Bighorn

THE FATE OF THE PLAINS INDIANS

issue 1

The Great Plains

the big picture

Key Question

- What were the Plains like?

The Great Plains were a desert as far as most Americans were concerned – at least until the mid-1800s. The area was judged to be uninhabitable by all except the native American Indians. In reality the Plains were a vast wilderness covering an enormous area of land as the map below shows.

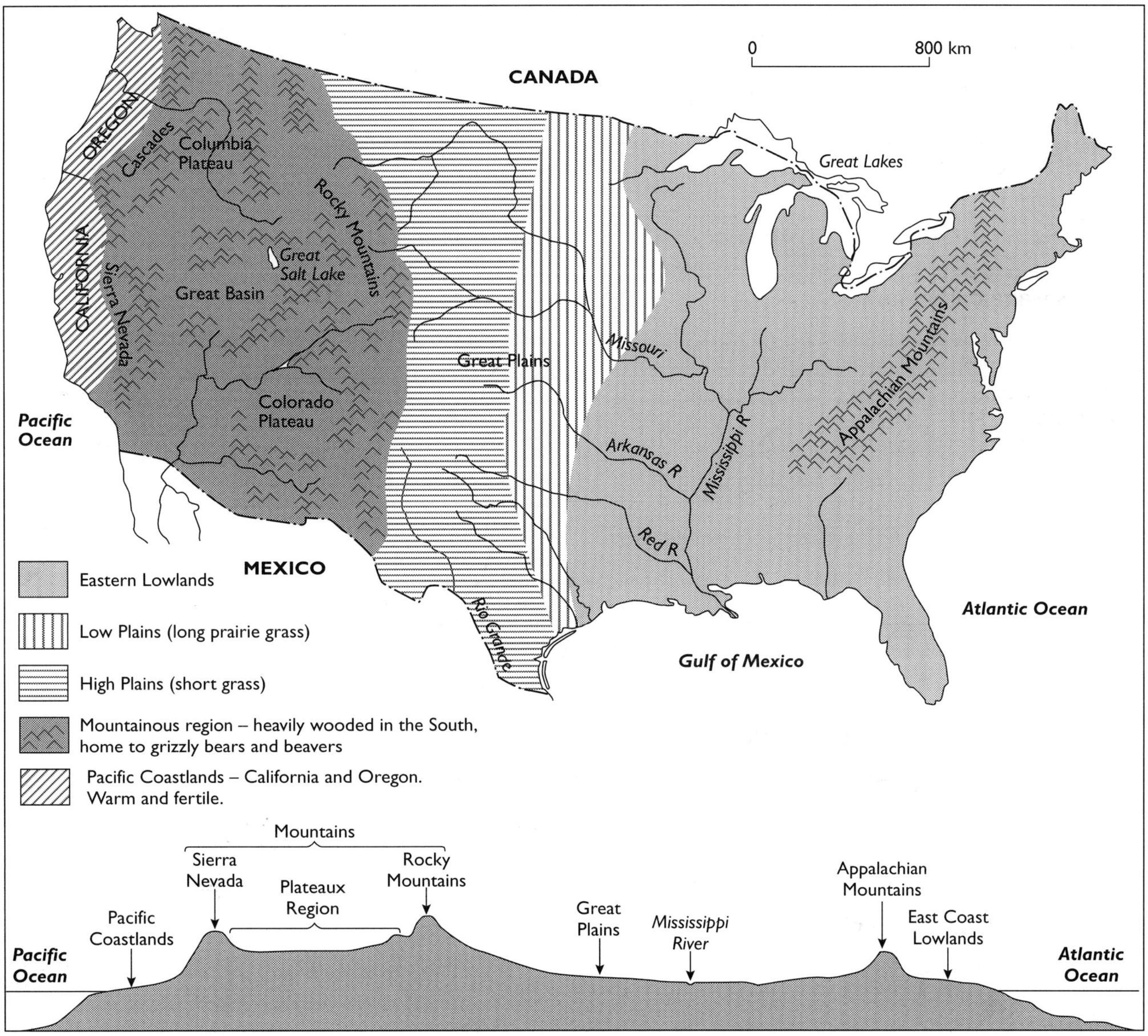

▲ *The geographical regions of the United States*

investigation 1.1 What were the Plains like?

The Great Plains remained unexplored until the mid-1800s. Early visitors declared that the area was uninhabitable – a view shared until at least 1820 as Source B (below) shows. Bordered to the east by the eastern lowlands, to the south by the Rio Grande river and to the west by the Rocky Mountains, the Plains represented a major obstacle to the settlement of the United States. As America gained more and more land in the west the Plains became a major obstacle separating the two sides of the country. With its unique climate and dominated by huge herds of buffalo the Plains appeared to many as an alien landscape. But some people did live there – and had done so successfully for between 25,000 and 40,000 years! The Indians of the Great Plains had adapted perfectly to their chosen environment.

SOURCE A

Much of the Plains was windswept and treeless, scorching in summer and freezing in winter. Until the 1850s it was called a desert, and a traveller would have seen a vast landscape with little but buffalo and sky, wild game and Indians. By 1890 this had all changed.

Derek Wise, *The American West*, 1984

SOURCE B

In regard to this extensive section of country, I do not hesitate in giving the opinion that it is almost wholly unfit for cultivation and of course uninhabitable by people depending on agriculture for their survival. The scarcity of wood and water will prove an insurmountable obstacle in the way of settling the west.

A report on the Plains by Major Stephen Long, 1819–20

SOURCE C

We did not think of the great open plains, the beautiful rolling hills and winding streams with tangled growth as 'wild'. To us it was tame. Earth was bountiful and we were surrounded with the blessings of the Great Spirit.

Luther Standing Bear, *My People the Sioux*

SOURCE D

No other part of America had such unpredictable weather or such extremes of temperature. The most constant weather feature of the Plains was the ferocious wind. In the summer the wind was scorching hot. In the winter the winds brought blizzards, tornadoes and hailstorms. Despite these extremes of climate, the Great Plains had many wild animals.

Schools History Project, *The American West*, 1974

things to do

Task 1:

1 Source A describes the Plains before 1890 but was not written until 1984. Does this mean that it must be unreliable?

2 Does Source B support Source A?

3 How useful is Source C to someone studying the Great Plains? Explain your answer.

4 Sources C and D give two impressions of the Great Plains. Why do you think they are so different?

things **to do**

Task 2:

Read the sources carefully. Complete the chart below by adding **positive** and **negative** comments.

Positive	**Negative**

Task 3:

Using the information from the sources, and your own knowledge, answer the following question:

What were the Great Plains like before 1850?

issue 2

The Plains Indians and their environment

the big picture

Key Questions

- How did the Indians adapt to life on the Plains?
- How did the Indians use the Plains?
- What were the Indians' attitudes to the land?
- How did the Indians use the buffalo?
- What were the Indians' attitudes to war and bravery?
- The Indian: noble Indian or savage barbarian?

The first Indians are thought to have entered North America between 25,000 and 40,000 years ago. During the Ice Age, when much of the sea was frozen, they are thought to have walked across the frozen Bering Straits between Russia and Alaska. Once in North America they spread out to colonise the whole continent. Each group of Indians developed a culture and lifestyle ideally suited to the land they chose to occupy.

The Great Plains were dominated by nomadic warrior tribes. To the north were the Blackfeet, Assiniboine and Crow peoples. In the central Plains were the Sioux and Cheyenne, while the Commanches, Kiowa and Arapaho dominated the southern Plains. The exact areas occupied by these tribes were constantly changing as a result of fighting among themselves and, later, as White expansion forced Indians from the east onto the Plains.

Some of the most powerful tribes, like the Sioux and the Cheyenne, had come to the Plains from the woodlands around the Great Lakes. These warrior peoples used horses to hunt buffalo and travelled the Plains following the great herds. Buffalo were also hunted by tribes like the Pawnee and Mandans. They lived mostly in permanent villages, farming the land around, and hunting buffalo in the summer months to supplement their diet and provide valuable raw materials.

In the south-west lived the Pueblo Indians. They lived in huge adobe (or mud-brick) apartment blocks and traded corn and horses with the nomadic tribes in return for buffalo robes. In the extreme south-west were the Apaches who had originally occupied the southern Plains but had been driven into the area of modern New Mexico by the powerful Commanches – probably the best horsemen on the Plains.

As pressure from White expansion grew in the 1840s many smaller tribes joined with the Whites against their traditional enemies.

Did you know?

There were around 300 different Indian languages spoken by North American Indians. To avoid confusion they developed a complex but very efficient sign language which was understood by all.

investigation 2.1 How did the Indians adapt to life on the Plains?

THE TEPEE

In order to survive on the Plains the Indians had to live off the land. Their most important source of food and raw materials was the buffalo. The Indians needed to be able to move about the Plains following the herds.

Before the arrival of the Europeans in the Americas there were no horses. The Indians used dogs to help them move their things around. The arrival of horses meant that the Indians could move further and faster. Their homes, the versatile tepee, could also be made larger because the horses could pull larger poles than the dogs they had used previously. Horses became a symbol of wealth and could be used for trade.

The tepee was built of 18- to 20-feet-long poles of stripped yellow pine. The diagram below shows how a tepee was erected.

1 Three poles were tied together to make a tripod. The tripod was stood upright. Other poles were placed against this frame. Once the structure was complete it was secured at the top.
2 The buffalo hide cover was tied to another pole which was then placed against the main structure.
3 The cover could then be unrolled around the tepee.
4 The cover was held at the front with wood or bone pegs (except for a space left for the entrance). Further pegs were used to stake the cover to the ground. The two remaining poles were then attached to the smoke flaps to control the size of the smoke hole.

Only two women (or older girls) would be required to erect a tepee. It was always women's work – but then, they did own the tepee! When a camp moved the poles were attached to either side of a horse. A frame between the two sets of poles could be used to carry the heavy hide tepee cover, elderly or infirm people or young children. This method of moving a tepee was called a travois. The diagram on the following sheet shows a travois in use.

▲ *The uses of a travois (note: even the dog pulls one!)*

Did you know?

A travois drawn by a horse could be used to carry a 300 lb (135 kg) load up to 12 miles (20 km) a day.

Did you know?

Many Indians did not bury their dead. Instead they wrapped the bodies in buffalo robes and placed them on tall platforms. Warriors had their weapons hung beside them, women had important household items.

things **to do**

- **Task 1:**
  Using the information about the tepee in this investigation, and your own knowledge, answer the following question:
  In what ways was the tepee perfectly suited to the Indian lifestyle?

Copy out the introductions set out below and use them to begin each new part of your answer.

To survive on the Plains the Indians needed to. . .

To do this they needed a home which could. . .

The tepee was perfectly suited to these needs because. . .

The harsh climate of the Plains with its fierce winds and extremes of temperature meant that the Indians had to build homes that were light and easy to move but strong enough to withstand the elements. The tepee was ideally suited. The frame could be erected or dismantled with relative ease in a matter of minutes. It was also easy to maintain. The temperature inside could be regulated yet the whole structure was strong and could easily withstand the punishing climate of the Plains.

SOURCE A

The tepee is much better to live in; always clean, warm in winter, cool in summer; easy to move. The White man builds big house, cost much money, like big cage, shut out sun, can never move; always sick. Indians and animals know better how to live than White men.

Chief Flying Hawk of the Sioux (1852[?]–1931)

SOURCE B

With smoke flaps for ventilation the tepee is cool in summer and, facing away from gales, is windproof in winter. In November the fire is moved inside and buffalo robes keep the occupants as cozy as beavers in their lodges.

***The Story of the Great American West*, 1977**

SOURCE D

The tepee of the Plains Indians is from 12 to 20 feet in diameter and 15 feet high. The fire is built in the centre and the smoke escapes through a hole at the top. The draught is, however, very defective and the tepee is usually, in cold weather, too full of smoke to be bearable to anyone but an Indian. The beds are piles of buffalo robes and blankets spread on the ground. They serve as a sleeping place by night, and seats by day. In this small space are often crowded eight or ten people. Since the cooking, eating, living and sleeping are all done in the one room, it soon becomes inconceivably filthy.

Colonel Dodge, a soldier on the Great Plains

SOURCE C

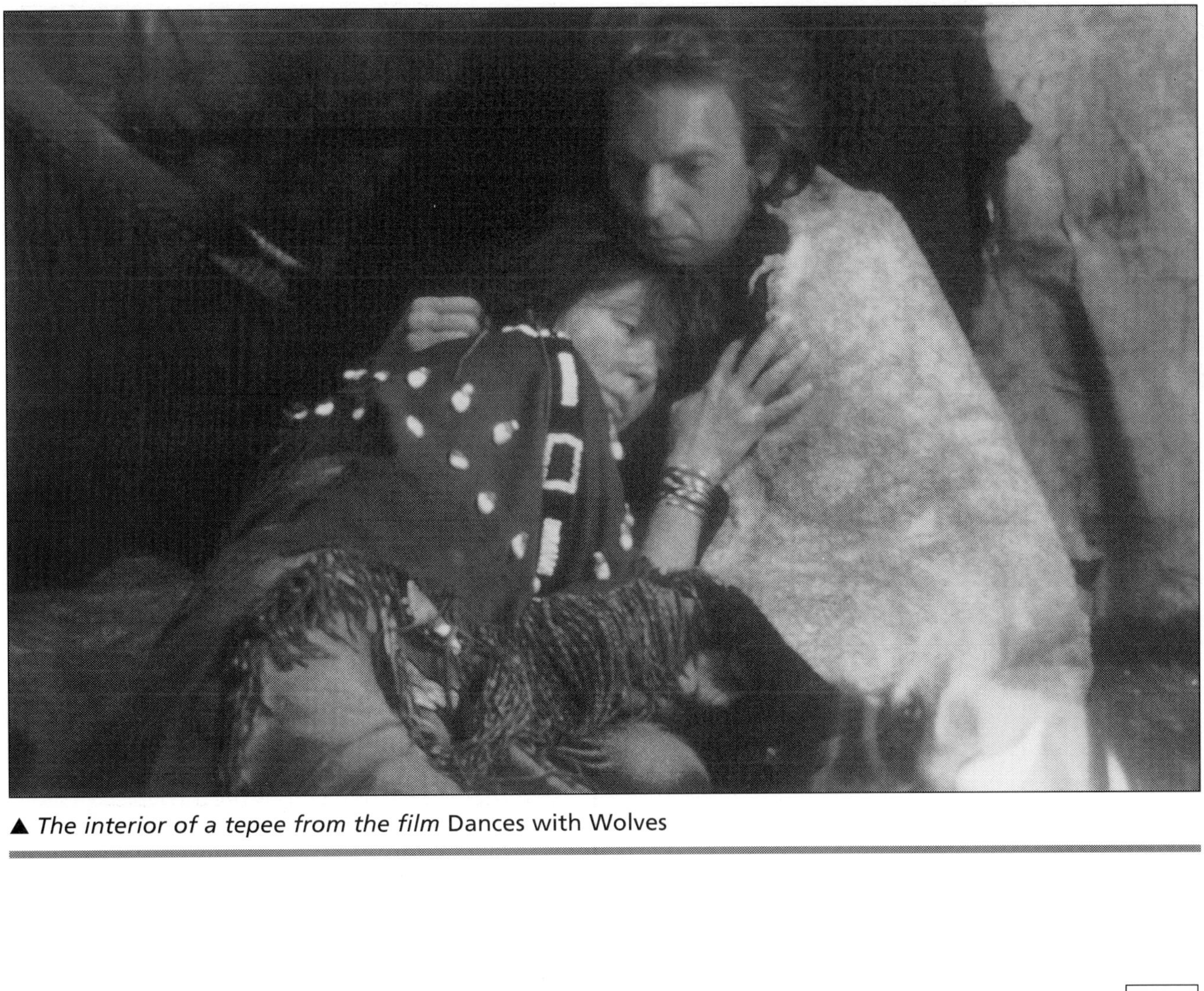

▲ *The interior of a tepee from the film* Dances with Wolves

things **to do**

Task 2:
Read and look at the sources on the previous page, which will tell you what some people thought about the tepee, then answer the following questions:

a What reasons does Chief Flying Hawk give in Source A to explain why the tepee is so much better than the White man's houses?

b Does Source B support Source A?

c Source C is a modern reconstruction of the inside of a tepee. Using Sources A and B do you think that Source C is reliable? Explain your answer.

d Source D was written by a White man. Does that make Source D unreliable? Explain your answer.

e Which source is the most useful for someone studying Indian tepees? Explain your answer.

▲ *Blackfoot tepees – note the elaborate designs which were often given to the owners in dreams (each had a special meaning)*

investigation 2.2 How did the Indians use the Plains?

The ground says 'It was the Great Spirit that placed me here. The Great Spirit tells me to take care of the Indians, to feed them right.'
Young Chief of the Cayuses, 1855

Did you know?

Indian medicine worked well for them but it had no answer for the diseases brought to America by the first Europeans. Smallpox and other diseases reduced the Indian population of 1.3 million in 1500 to a population of only 400,000 before it picked up again.

The plants of the Great Plains provided the Indians with food, raw materials, medicines and items for their ceremonies.

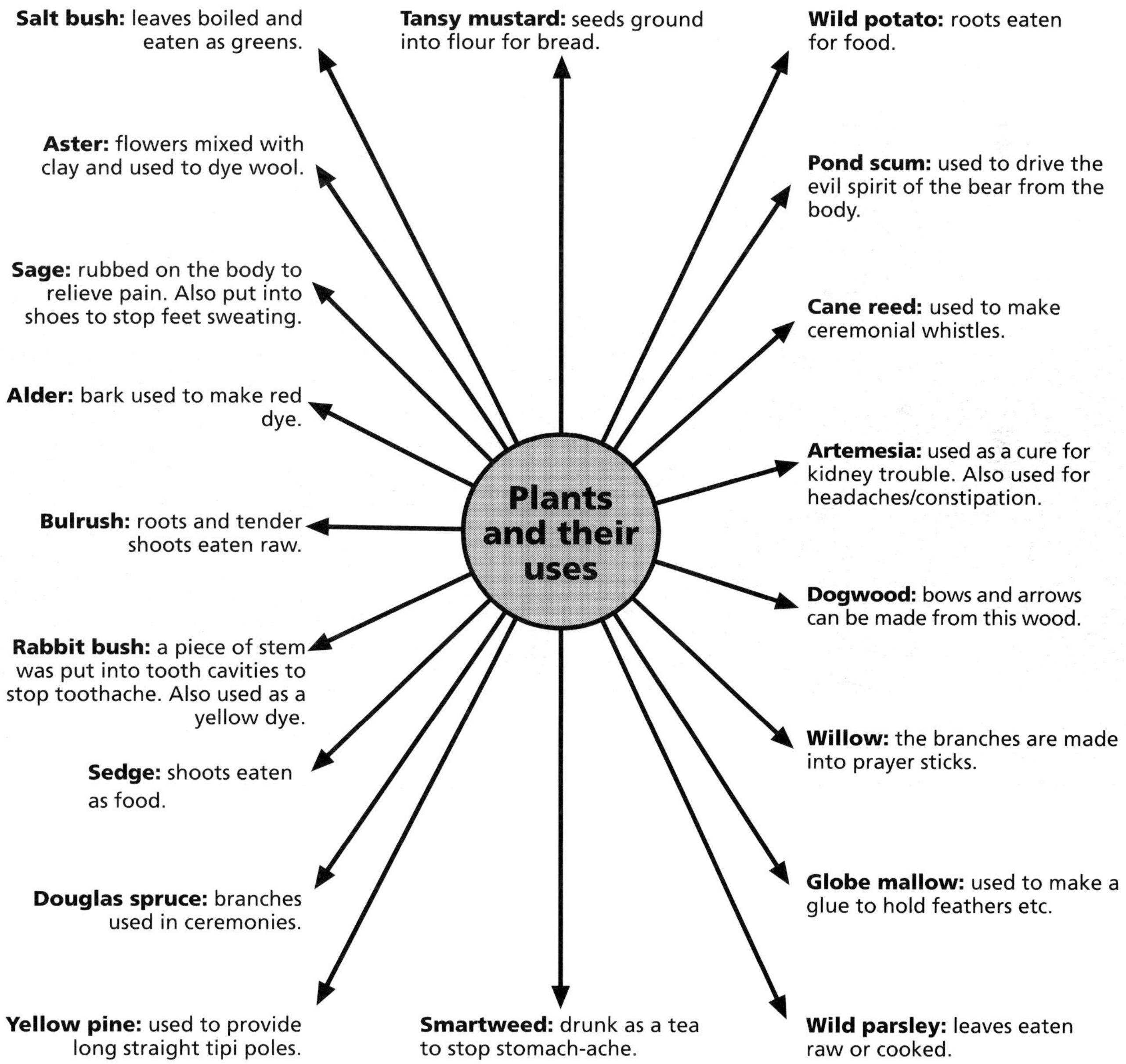

things **to do**

Task 1:
The diagram on the previous page shows a number of plants used by the Plains Indians, but there were many more. Look at each plant named and try to decide whether it provided *food, medicine, raw materials* or *items for ceremonies*. When you have decided, complete the chart below by adding the name of the plant in the appropriate column.

Food	Raw materials	Medicines	Ceremonial

Task 2:
Using the information from task 1, and your own knowledge, answer the following question:
Chief Young Child believed that The Great Spirit told the ground to provide for the Indians.
Do you think that the ground was successful? Explain your answer.

Did you know?

Indian medicine men were aware of caffeine as a stimulant and the pain-relieving effects of salycylic acid (aspirin).

investigation 2.3 What were the Indians' attitudes towards the land?

Investigations 2.1 and 2.2 have shown how important the land was to Indian survival. Unable to explain much of what happened around them (why storms occurred, why the rains did not come, why thunder crashed etc.) they came to see the earth as a very spiritual place. When things did not go well it was assumed that the spirits were angry. To prevent this from happening the Indians paid particular attention to pleasing the spirits both by individual acts and by dances and ceremonies involving many people. The following sources explain some of their beliefs:

SOURCE A

Holy Mother Earth, the trees and all nature are witnesses of your thoughts and deeds.

A Winnebago wise saying

SOURCE B

The Lakota (Sioux) loved the earth. Their tepees were built upon the earth. The birds that flew in the air came to rest upon the earth and it was the final resting place of all things that lived and grew. Kinship with all creatures of the earth, sky and water was a real and active principle. The old Sioux was wise. He knew that man's heart away from nature becomes hard.

Chief Luther Standing Bear of the Oglala Sioux

SOURCE C

The average Indian of the Plains is a being who does little credit to human nature. As I passed over the magnificent lands of Kansas which form the reservations of the Delawares, Potawotomies etc. – the very best cornlands on earth – and saw their owners sitting around the doors of their tepees at the height of the planting season, I could not help saying 'These people must die out – there is no help for them. God has given this earth to those who will subdue and cultivate it'.

Horace Greeley, an eastern newspaper editor, who travelled from New York to San Francisco in 1859

SOURCE D

The ground says 'It is the Great Spirit that placed me here. The Great Spirit tells me to take care of the Indians; to feed them right. The Great Spirit made the roots to feed the Indians on'. The water says the same thing. 'The Great Spirit tells me "Feed the Indians well" '. The ground says the same thing. The ground says 'The Great Spirit has placed me here to produce all that grows on me. It was from me that man was made'. The Great Spirit in placing man on the earth wanted them to take good care of the ground.

Young Chief of the Cayuses, 1855

SOURCE E

I looked at the land and the rivers, the sky above, and the animals around me and I could not fail to realise that they were made by some great power. Then I had a dream, and in my dream I was told that the maker of all was the Great Spirit (Wakan tanka) and that in order to honour him I must honour his work in nature.

Brave Buffalo of the Sioux

SOURCE F

My father sent for me. I saw that he was dying. He said 'My son, never forget my dying words. This country holds your father's body. Never sell the bones of your father and your mother'. I buried him in that beautiful valley. I love that land more than all the rest of the world. A man who would not love his father's grave is worse than a wild animal.

Chief Joseph of the Nez Perces

Did you know?

Many Indians believed that all power came from the Great Spirit. They would sing to attract the Spirit's help. This would come in the form of a vision which would give the Indian sacred power. Those who gained the greatest power often went on to become medicine men.

SOURCE G

◀ *An Indian prays to the Great Spirit*

things **to do**

Task 1:

Look at Sources A to G in this investigation and answer the following questions:

a What is Source A trying to say?

b What reasons do Sources B and D give to explain why the Indians regarded the earth as sacred?

c Source E refers to Brave Buffalo's dream. As it is about a dream, the source must be unreliable. Do you agree? Explain you answer.

d How useful is Source G as evidence of Indian religion?

e Does Source F support Source B? Explain your answer.

f Why do you think that the Indians were 'sitting around the doors of their tepees at the height of the planting season' as stated in Source C?

Task 2:

God has given this earth to those who will subdue and cultivate it.

Use the information from the sources, and your own knowledge, to explain how an Indian might have replied to this view.

investigation 2.4 How did the Indians use the buffalo?

The buffalo was the key to Indian survival on the Great Plains. Buffalo roamed the Plains in large herds, which the Indians followed. These huge animals could provide almost everything the Indians needed – and nothing was wasted!

These sources explain how the buffalo were used:

SOURCE A

With the hides they make their houses and they make clothes and shoes. They make rope from the hair. From the tendons they make thread which they use to sew their clothes and their tepee covers. From the bones they make tools, and the dung is used as fuel because there is no wood in that country. The stomachs, bladders and intestines are used as containers and vessels from which they drink. They eat the meat.

A Spanish traveller in 1540

Did you know?

Before 1800 there were estimated to be between 50 and 150 million buffalo on the Plains. In 1900 there were 541!

SOURCE B

No part of the buffalo was ever wasted. Fresh buffalo meat was roasted and eaten or it could be dried and stored for the winter. The brains, liver and fat were used to tan the hides. The tongue was either eaten or dried for use as a hairbrush. Raw hide was tough and used for shoe soles, boxes and harnesses whereas the softer tanned hide was used for tepee covers, bags and clothes. The fur was used for blankets and even the hair could be used to stuff pillows and saddles. The hooves were made into bowls or boiled to make glue. The shoulder blades made useful shovels. Even the skull was used in ceremonies to release the buffalo's spirit. The horns could be made into drinking cups.

Adapted from Paul Steele, *The Environment Of the Plains Indians*, 1986

SOURCE C

The buffalo supplies the Indians with the necessities of life – with a home, food, clothing, beds and fuel; strings for their bows, glue, thread, trail ropes and for the horses, saddle covers, water containers, boats and the means to trade with White traders. When the buffalo are extinct, the Indian too must die away.

Francis Parkman, *The Oregon Trail*, 1840s

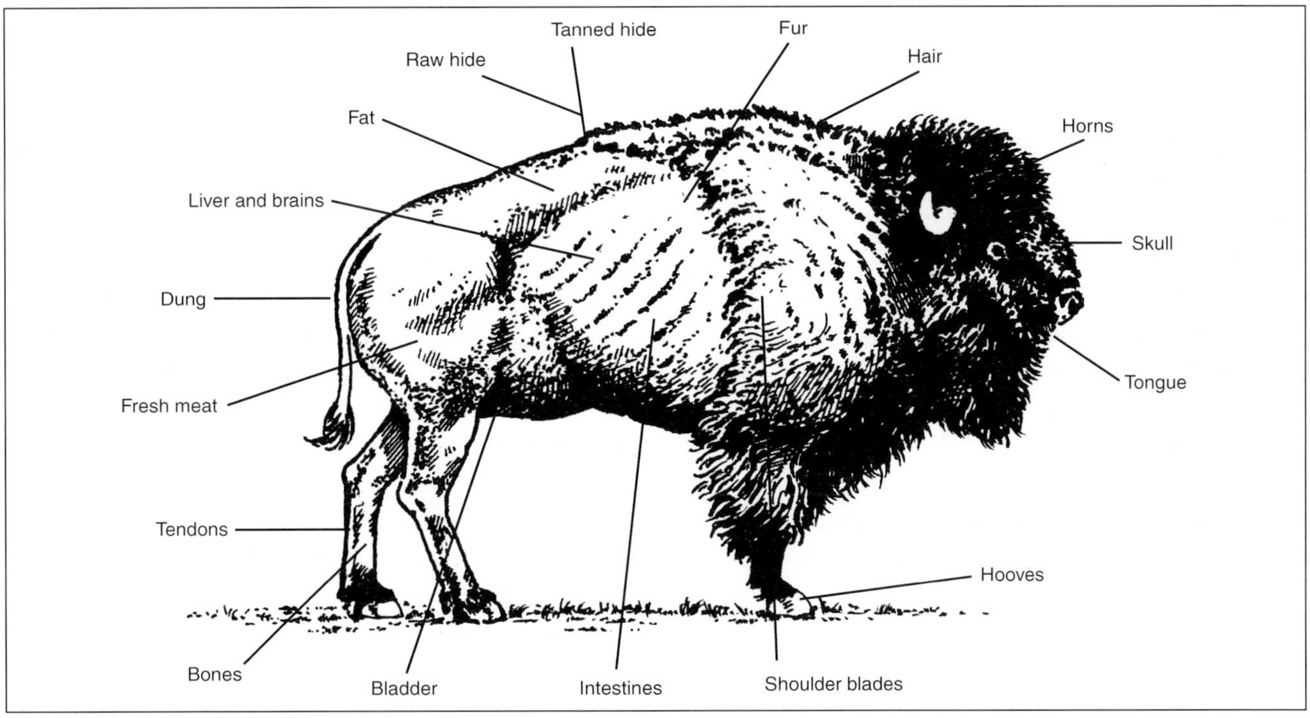

things **to do**

Task 1:
Using the information from the sources on the previous page, and your own knowledge, complete the chart below.

Parts of the buffalo	What it was used for
horns	
intestines	
skull	
bones	
tongue	
bladder	
fur	
hair	
hooves	
dung	
fresh meat	
liver and brains	
fat	
raw hide	
tanned hide	
tendons	
shoulder blades	

things **to do**

Task 2:

Complete the diagram below by adding the different parts of the buffalo, and the product made, to the appropriate section. One example has already been added to help you.

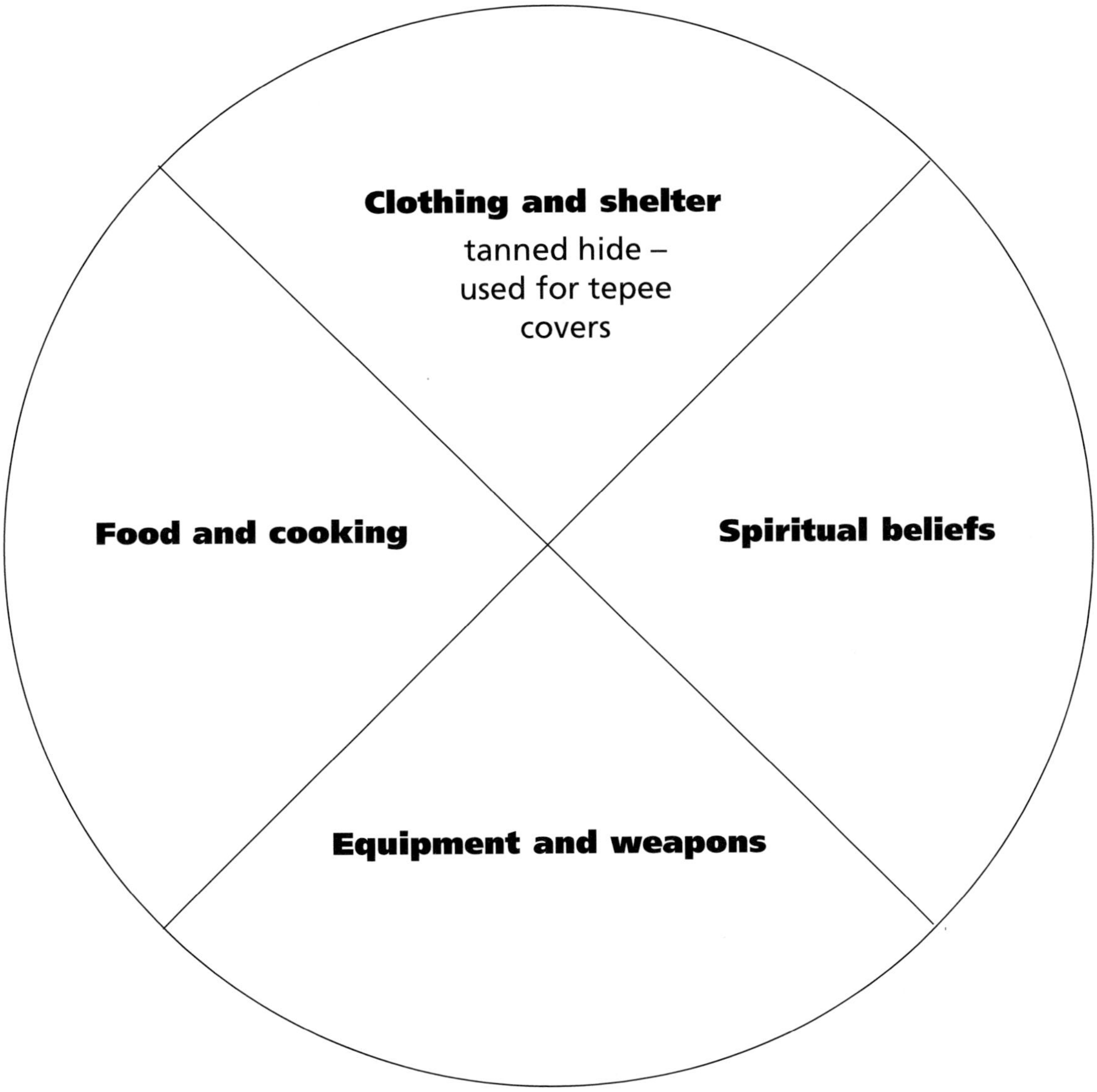

Task 3:

The buffalo hunters have done more to end the Indian problem in two years than the entire army has done in the last thirty years.

General P Sheridan, US Army

Fact: Between 1872 and 1874 alone 3,158,730 buffalo were killed by White hunters; 1,378,359 buffalo skins were collected – the rest were left to rot.

Using the information collected in tasks 1 and 2 in this investigation explain why the buffalo hunters mentioned by General Sheridan had been so important in defeating the Indians.

What were the Indians' attitudes to war and bravery?

Many Whites regarded Indians as cowards who would run away rather than fight, and who preferred ambushes and surprise attacks to pitched battles.

> There is in every Indian a total lack of that courage which prompts men to fight from a sense of duty. This is because of his lack of that shoulder to shoulder courage which comes with discipline.
>
> **Colonel Dodge, 1877**

> The first impulse of the Indian when surprised in his camp is that most natural to all animals – to scuttle away as fast as his legs will carry him. The Indians very rarely meet a charge – their army melts away.
>
> **Colonel Dodge, 1877**

We tend to think of Custer's Last Stand and the battle of Rorkes's Drift (as seen in the film *Zulu*) as heroic, but most Indians would not agree. To die a gallant death when escape was possible was considered selfish. Each warrior left behind a tepee full of women and children dependent on them for food and protection. It was considered far better to run away and return to fight another day.

That is not to say that the Indians were not brave. Bravery was encouraged among the Indians, and publicly rewarded by a system known as counting coups. Warriors would attempt brave deeds in the hope that their bravery would be noticed. If that happened, they would be awarded an eagle feather reflecting their achievements. Many warriors collected these feathers and attached them to headdresses – the famous feathered bonnets seen in the westerns. In reality many warriors boasted splendid feathered bonnets, not just chiefs.

To kill an enemy in combat was considered brave but it did not rank as highly as touching a live enemy and withdrawing. Some warriors went into battle armed only with long, hooked lances known as coup sticks in order to touch their enemies.

The Omaha Indians had six levels of honour and bravery:

1 The highest honour was striking an unwounded enemy with the hand, bow or coup stick.
2 Striking a wounded enemy.
3 Striking (with bow, hand or coup stick) the body of a dead enemy.
4 Killing an enemy.
5 Taking a scalp (although this often became number 4 since it was usually necessary to kill an enemy in order to remove their scalp).
6 Severing the head from the body of a dead enemy.

Most other tribes had similar levels of bravery. Even the feathers which were awarded could be cut or decorated to reflect the level of bravery shown.

Bravery was also a way of appeasing the spirits. In the Sun Dance ceremony warriors would have wooden or bone skewers inserted behind the muscles of the chest or back. They would then be attached to leather cords and suspended until the muscles tore. While this was clearly accepted as a measure of bravery no one was compelled to undergo the Sun Dance. One of the most famous and successful chiefs, Crazy Horse, never did the dance whereas Sitting Bull did it several times.

Did you know?

During the American Civil War (1861–5) many Indians actually fought either for the North or the South. The Cherokees, Creeks, Choctaws, Chickasaws and Seminoles joined the South. They were good fighters but tended to scalp their victims. After the Battle of Pea Ridge the Cherokees built a fire around a captured cannon. It was loaded and soon exploded with the heat killing some Indians and ending the festivities!

Did you know?

Some Indian warriors were known as contraries because they did everything backwards. They would ride their horses backwards, laugh instead of cry, wash in dirt, flee instead of attack and so on.

▲ The Sun Dance *by Frederick Remington, 1890*

things **to do**

- **Task 1:**
  You have read Colonel Dodge's comments on the Indians. He is firmly of the opinion that the Indians are cowards.

  Using the information in this investigation, and your own knowledge, consider how you would answer him. You need to explain that the Indians were not cowards but simply had a different set of values.

  The suggested sentence beginnings in the box below might help you write your answer.

Colonel Dodge says that . . .

The Indians *were* brave. They showed their bravery by . . .

The Indians also used bravery as . . .

The Indians did not stand and fight like Whites because . . .

investigation 2.6 The role of women and children in Indian society

Indian men and women had very clear – and different – jobs to do. Women were needed to maintain the home, raise the children, and prepare the food while the men were needed to act as providers and proctectors.

The Blackfeet Indians explained how this came about:

> Men and women emerged from two different lakes and for some time they lived separately. The men, however, were poor and naked since they did not know how to tan hides. The women suffered because they had no skill in hunting. The Great Spirit brought the two sexes together. This proved so successful that it was decided to make it permanent.
>
> **19th century Blackfeet legend**

Although it might appear that the women actually had very little power, in reality they had a considerable amount. They owned the family home and effectively controlled the distribution of food. They had a great deal of say in their choice of partner (although arranged marrriages were not unknown) and in the question of divorce.

Women also had an important voice in the making of decisions in the family and in the band. Although women rarely sat in on council meetings few men would form an opinion without considering the views of their wives.

The praise or contempt of women was also important in a warrior's life. After a successful raid warriors were praised with songs and dances but if a warrior was unsuccessful he could be ignored and humiliated until he was able to prove himself at a later date.

Women were also responsible for preparing the buffalo hides, cooking, making clothing and decorating finished items with beadwork and/or quills. In the 1850s the Indian trader Edwin Denig noted that 'When the buffalo are plentiful anyone can kill. The raw hide of an animal has no value. It is the labour of making it into a robe or skin fit for sale or use that makes it valuable. Women, therefore, are the greatest wealth an Indian possesses.'

Although women had a limited role in Indian politics, they had a far greater role in religion. Women's societies performed a number of important ceremonies (for example linked with buffalo calling and producing food). Women also played an important role in the sun-dance ceremonies. Among the Blackfeet the ceremony was led by a woman.

The key to a woman's power lay in her ability to bear children. This gave her the power of life and, therefore, control over the future existence of the people. The birth of a child was a cause for great celebration.

As Robert Higheagle of the Sioux noted in the 1890s, 'It is strictly believed and understood by the Sioux that a child is the greatest gift from Wakan Tanka [the Great Spirit] in response to many prayers and promises.'

Plains children were treated with great tenderness and rarely punished as the traveller Francis Parkman recorded in 1840. 'Most Indians were very fond of their children, whom they never punished except in extreme cases, when they threw a bowl of cold water over them.'

Children were usually born in their mother's tepee. Most women would only have two or three children – usually with a few years between them to allow each child to be nursed through infancy. However, the Plains were a very harsh place for children and 'not more than two out of five children live until youth is over'. (Trader Edwin Denig writing in the 1850s).

Soon after birth each child would receive a name (although they would rarely keep this name). These early names usually reflected a characteristic of the child. As a child Sitting Bull was seen to always look carefully at food before eating it. As a result he was named Hunkeshne (meaning 'slow' or 'thoughtful'). When he struck his first enemy his father renamed him Tatanka Iyotake (meaning Sitting Bull to reflect the courage of the buffalo bull). Children could also be given the name of an aged relative. Since that person had lived so long they clearly had the favour of the spirits and, therefore, use of the name might pass that fortune onto the young child.

As they grew older, boys and girls played separately so as to learn the skills they would need in life. Buffalo Bird of the Hidatsa (born in around 1850) recalled that her mother told her 'if

▲ *A photograph showing Indian girls playing with miniature tepees. This taught them how to erect and dismantle a tepee and how to control the smoke flaps*

you play with girls you will grow up to be a woman.' Girls played with toys which echoed the things used in the family home. They carried dolls in miniature cradle boards (packs which were carried on the mother's back and which held the baby firmly strapped in), and played with model tepees and travois. The boys, meanwhile, played mock battles and learned the skills of horse riding. Most Indian boys were skilled at bareback horse riding by the age of five or six.

The Sioux looked for four qualities in a woman – bravery, honesty, generosity and childbearing. The Cree saw childbearing as so important that they used the same word for 'mother' and 'woman'. However, above all, a girl's chastity was most important. As a result, as a girl became older she began to lose her freedom. Increasingly older brothers or other relatives would accompany her everywhere to protect her from the interests of other men and so protect her chastity ready for marriage.

things **to do**

- **Task 1:**
  - a Read the information in this investigation and list the various things which women were expected to do.
  - b Explain how these responsibilities gave women power in an Indian band.
- **Task 2:**
  Explain what lessons Indian boys and girls learned and why.
- **Task 3:**
  Using the information from this investigation, and your own knowledge, answer the following question:

  Indian children had no education.
  Do you agree? Explain your answer.

  The suggested sentence beginnings below might help you write your answer.

Indian education

In order for the Indians to survive, children needed to learn . . .

They learned these skills from their parents who began to teach them . . .

Boys and girs learned different things because . . .

Therefore, it is not true to say that Indian children received no education because . . .

investigation 2.7 The Indian: noble Indian or savage barbarian?

Here are a number of sources that give different views of the Indians. Some are from the Indians themselves; others are from White men with different experiences of the Indians.

SOURCE A

The head man went around picking out the best hunters. To these he said 'Young warriors, today you will feed the helpless. You shall help the old and the young. Whatever you kill shall be theirs.'

Black Elk, a Sioux holy man

SOURCE B

▲ *An extract from a modern children's comic*

SOURCE C

▲ *A White view of an Indian taking a White man's scalp, 1892*

SOURCE D

The Indians are children. Their wars, treaties and homes all belong to the lowest levels of human life. Proud and worthless, lazy and lousy they will strut out, or drink out, their miserable lives and, eventually, do the world a favour by dying out of it.

Horace Greeley (an east coast newspaper editor) after a journey across America, 1859

SOURCE E

The Injuns will catch you while crossing the Plains,
they'll kill you and scalp you and beat out your brains.
Uncle Sam ought to throw them all over the fence,
so there'll be no Red Indians a 100 years hence.

Anonymous rhyme from the 1870s

SOURCE F

▲ *A White cartoon which appeared after the Battle of the Little Bighorn, 1876*

SOURCE G

I could not have believed we could have travelled so far with so little difficulty. The Indians frequently came to see us. All were so friendly that I cannot help feeling sympathy and friendship for them.

George Donner, leader of a wagon train heading for California, 1846

SOURCE H

Our land is more valuable than your money. We cannot sell the lives of men and animals; therefore we cannot sell this land. It was put here for us by the Great Spirit and we cannot sell it because it does not belong to us.

A Blackfoot Chief comparing White and Indian attitudes to the land

SOURCE I

The more we can kill this year, the less will have to be killed next year. For the more I see of these Indians the more convinced I am that all have to be killed, or kept as paupers [poor people].

General W Sherman, US Military Commander on the Great Plains

SOURCE J

I have heard it said that the Indians have no religion but only ignorant superstition. I say to you that the Indian is a highly moral and religious person.

George Catlin, an artist who lived with the Indians

things **to do**

Task 1:

Look at the sources and decide which are *for* the Indians and which are *against*. When you have decided, complete the chart below.

For	Against

Task 2:

Now look at the type and origins of each source. (Origins mean who said or wrote it.) Enter the source type and/or author of each source in the appropriate place in the chart above (e.g. a cartoon produced by Whites). What patterns emerge?

Task 3:

Using the information from tasks 1 and 2, and your own knowledge, answer the following question:

Francis Boller (a White man who knew the Indians well) wrote: 'So it always is. The more ignorant people are of the Indians' lifestyle and warfare, the more they appear to despise them.'

Do you agree? Explain your answer.

issue 3

The reasons for White settlement on the Plains

the **big** picture

Key Question

- Why did people move onto the Plains?

Many different groups of people moved onto the Plains in the second half of the nineteenth century. There were trappers, farmers, miners and many others. Their reasons for moving west were often as different as the people themselves but they all shared a belief in the principle of manifest destiny.

Before 1840 the US Government had no real interest in the Great Plains and regarded the area as simply a desert, unfit for anything except the Indians. However, the opening up of new tracts of land on the west coasts and in Texas began to change their mind.

The question was how to take the lands from the Indians. The answer was 'manifest destiny'. The idea was explained to the American people by John O'Sullivan (editor of the *New York Morning News*) in 1845.

> It is our manifest destiny to spread over and possess the whole of the American continent which God has given us for the development of the great experiment of liberty.

A belief in the idea of 'manifest destiny' was to be the key to taming the Plains. It could be used to

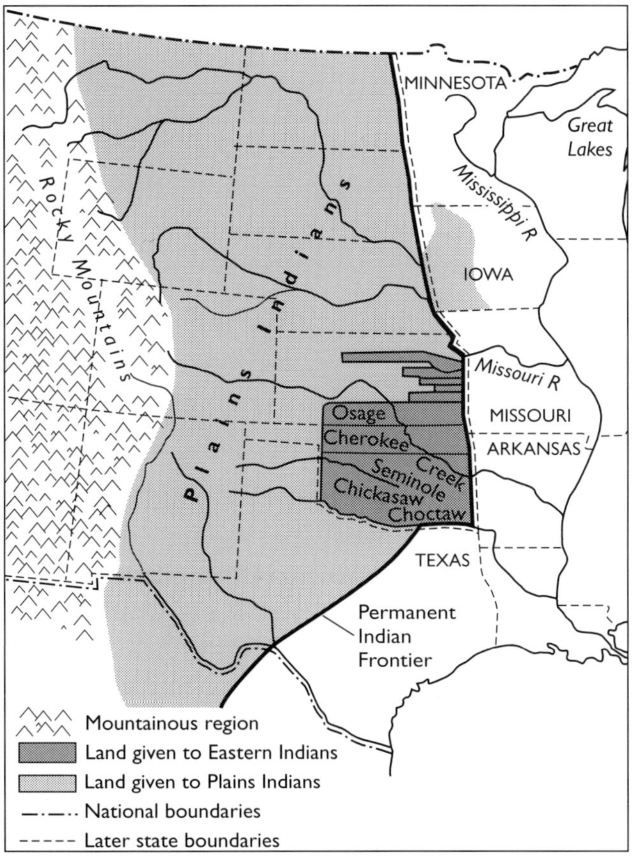

▲ *Indian lands on the Great Plains in 1840*

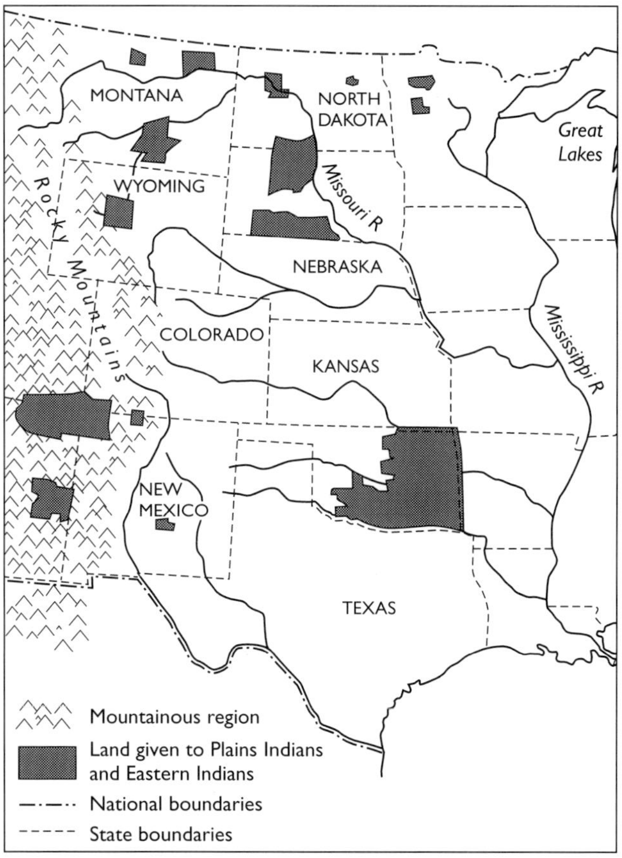

▲ *Indian lands on the Great Plains in 1900*

justify the seizure of any land as another New York newspaper editor explained:

> There is no such thing as title of ownership to the wild lands of the new world [i.e. the Plains] other than that given by actual possession.

As to who that owner should be, Horace Greeley (another newspaper editor) was in no doubt:

> God has given this earth to those who will subdue and cultivate it.

The maps on the previous page show just how enthusiastically the American people embraced the idea of 'manifest destiny'.

Did you know?

Between 1835 and 1855 10,000 pioneers died along the Oregon Trail. Of these only perhaps 400 died from Indian attacks. The rest died of diseases like cholera and smallpox.

investigation 3.1 Why did people move onto the Plains?

The reasons why people moved onto the Plains can be divided into two groups:

- **Push factors:** things which push people out of where they are already living;
- **Pull factors:** things which pull people into another area.

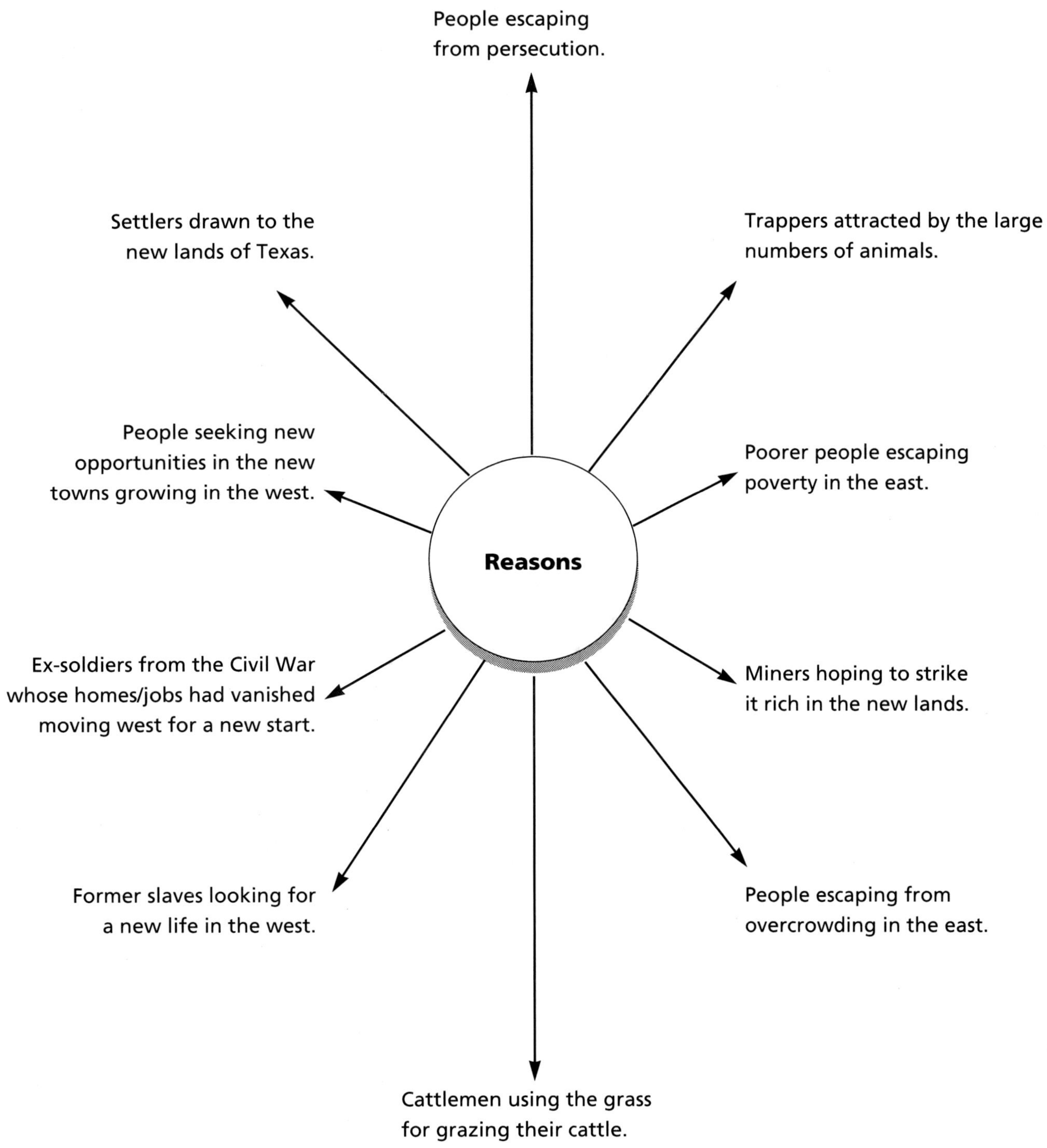

things **to do**

- **Task 1:**
Look at the reasons given on the previous page which explain why many people moved onto the Great Plains. There are other reasons too – for example, escaping from the law!

Decide which of the reasons are *push factors* and which are *pull factors* and add them to the chart below.

- **Task 2:**
Use the information from task 1, and your own knowledge, to answer the following question:
Why did White people move to the Great Plains?

Push factors	Pull factors

Did you know?

Some travellers across the Plains took the strangest things with them which they were later forced to abandon. One traveller recorded seeing a steel safe and a diving bell! In 1850 a man crossing the Carson Desert counted the remains of 2,381 horses and mules, 433 oxen, 787 wagons and goods worth $100,000!

The Mormons and Salt Lake City

issue 4

the **big** picture

Key Questions

- Why did the Mormons move to the Great Salt Lake?
- How important was Brigham Young to the Mormons?
- What was the Great Salt Lake like?
- How well did the Mormons cope at the Great Salt Lake?

The Mormon Church (or Church of Jesus Christ of the Latter Day Saints) was founded by Joseph Smith in June 1830. Smith claimed that, as a boy of 17, he was visited by an angel called Moroni. According to Smith's story, the angel told him to dig on a hillside where he discovered a set of gold plates. When Smith was finally allowed to remove the plates (some four years later) he found them covered in a strange writing. With the aid of a set of crystal spectacles, Smith read the story on the plates.

The story told of the tribes of Israel who had travelled to America where they began to fight among themselves. The fighting continued until Christ appeared in America. Later, the fighting started again, ending with the Battle of Cumorah (around AD 384). Among the survivors were Mormon and his son Moroni. They spent the rest of their lives writing the story of their people on the plates. Whoever found the plates was ordered to build up the church in America and elsewhere before Christ returned.

In March 1830 Joseph Smith published the story as *The Book of Mormon* (after Mormon, father of Moroni). Within a year of the book's publication there were over a thousand Mormons. In 1831 Smith chose the town of Kirtland, Ohio, as the new City of God.

Sadly, relations between the Mormons and their neighbours soon deteriorated and the Mormons were forced to leave for their own safety. After the death of Smith at the hands of an angry mob their new leader, Brigham Young, led them across the Plains to the Great Salt Lake.

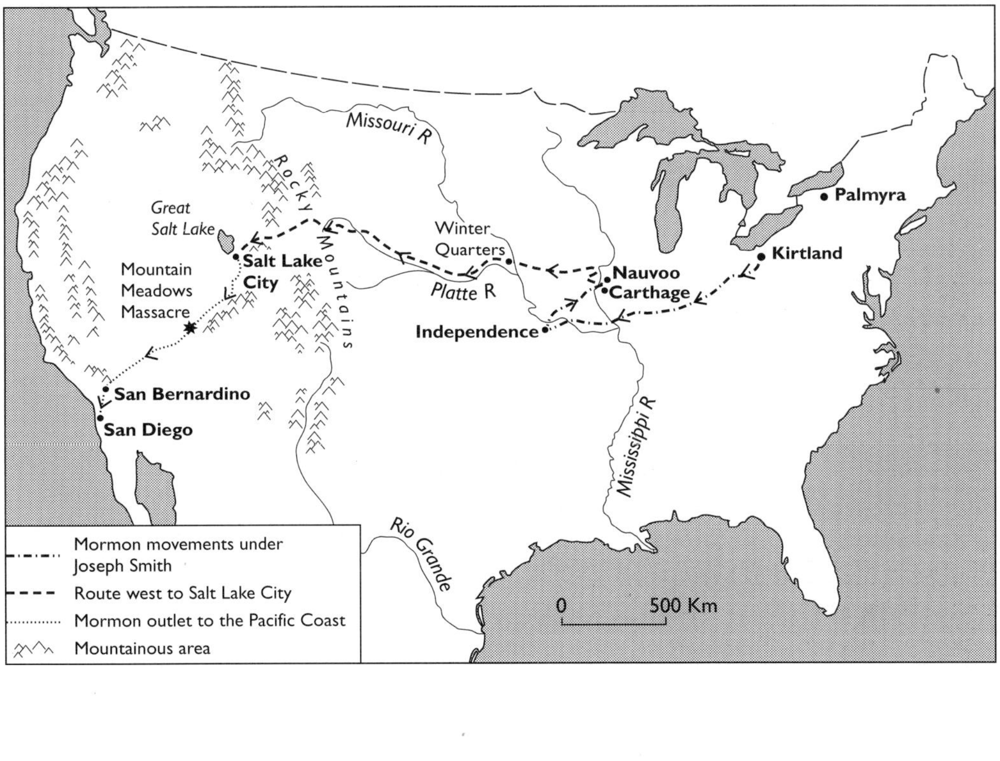

◀ *The movements and settlements of the Mormons*

Did you know?

The Mormon Church is the fastest growing church in Britain today.

investigation 4.1 Why did the Mormons move to the Great Salt Lake?

The Mormons moved to the Great Salt Lake because they were hated by the non-Mormons (whom they called gentiles). When Joseph Smith was murdered by an anti-Mormon mob they knew they would have to find a new home. There are many reasons why the Mormons were forced to leave their homes, as the diagram below shows.

Did you know?

The Mormon's trail west to the Great Salt Lake was so well marked that the Pony Express riders used parts of it on their journey to California.

Why the Mormons were unpopular

- Joseph Smith ran for President of the United States. People feared that this would give the Mormons more power.
- Smith founded a bank which collapsed causing debts for many non-Mormons.
- The Mormons accused their non-Mormon neighbours of theft, racing and gambling. This made the Mormons unpopular.
- Non-Mormons were afraid of the Mormon secret army known as the 'Danites'.
- Non-Mormons were afraid of Mormon sympathy for the Indians.
- The Mormons worked hard and became prosperous. Poorer non-Mormons were jealous.
- The Mormons opposed slavery but many of their neighbours had slaves. This made Mormons unpopular.
- Mormon leaders had religious and political power which was feared by non-Mormons.
- The Mormons wanted their own laws which made them appear different.
- Mormons called themselves 'Chosen People' and said that only they would go to heaven. This angered non-Mormons.
- The Mormons practised polygamy (i.e. they had more than one wife) and non-Mormons hated this.
- The Mormons wanted to convert as many people as possible to the Mormon Church. This worried non-Mormons who feared being taken over.

things **to do**

- **Task 1:**
  Look at the reasons given on the previous page to explain the unpopularity of the Mormons. Decide whether each reason is:
- **political:** to do with running a town or country;
- **religious:** to do with peoples' religious beliefs;
- **social:** to do with the way people live and work together;
- **economic:** to do with money;

and add it to the chart below.

Political	Religious	Social	Economic

things **to do**

- **Task 2:**

  Look at the pictures below. These show different acts of violence against the Mormons. Using the information from task 1, and your own knowledge, answer the following question:

  Why would non-Mormons want to attack the Mormons?

- **Task 3:**

  Having decided to move away to avoid further acts of violence the new leader, Brigham Young, chose the Great Salt Lake as the new Mormon home. The area was desolate and uninhabited. It was also outside US Government control, being part of Mexico.

  Using the information from tasks 1 and 2, and your own knowledge, answer the following question:

  Why did the Mormons move to the Great Salt Lake?

▲ *An attack on Mormons at Haun's Mill*

▲ *The murder of Joseph Smith at Carthage*

▲ *Mormons being tarred and feathered*

▲ *Mormons being beaten up by mobs*

investigation 4.2 How important was Brigham Young to the Mormons?

After the murder of Joseph Smith, the Mormons were a leaderless and threatened community. In 1844 Brigham Young became the new leader of the Mormon Church. He realised that the Mormons could not survive in Illinois and would have to move. But where? What was needed was a place far away from US Government interference where the Mormons could live alone without having to endure the hatred of their neighbours. The southern part of the Rocky Mountains offered such a place – it was desolate and forbidding, largely uninhabited and belonged to Mexico. On 9 August 1846 the Mormons told US President Polk of their decision to move there.

The decision to move to the southern Rockies was a very brave one. To be successful they would have to overcome many problems . . .

PROBLEMS AND SOLUTIONS

Brigham Young took control of 15,000 Mormons. The journey to the Great Salt Lake (part of the southern Rockies) was over 2,250 kms. There were no roads or shops along the way so the Mormons had to provide everything that they would need on the journey – even the wagons! Young set everyone to work making wagons and preparing supplies. Meanwhile, attacks on the Mormons were becoming so bad that the Mormons were forced to leave before they were ready.

Sources A and B show the effects of the rush to leave:

SOURCE A

The fever was present to such an extent that hardly anyone escaped it. Even the cows went unmilked. Burials were slow and you might see women sat in the open tents keeping the flies off their dead children some time after decomposition had set in.

Thomas Kane, a US Army doctor who gave medical help to the Mormons

SOURCE B

We were poorly prepared for our journey and many joining us had little or nothing, so our meagre rations had to be divided among them. We had weeks of cold stormy weather. Our oxen were not strong enough to pull the loads so travelling was next to an impossibility. We were put on rations. During that time our biscuits went mouldy.

RS Howells, a Mormon who made the journey from Illinois

Despite these problems Young never gave up. Instead he took measures to overcome the problems as the following sources show:

SOURCE C: PIONEER COMPANIES

In March a company of pioneers, mostly young, strong men, will set out. The object of this move is to put in a spring crop, to build houses, and to prepare to receive families who will start off as soon as the grass is grown enough to feed the animals.

Brigham Young, writing in a Mormon circular to let people know what was happening

SOURCE D: DISCIPLINE ON THE MARCH

At 5.00 am the bugle is to be sounded to tell every man to arise and attend prayers. Then cooking, eating, feeding oxen etc. till 7.00 at which time the camp is to move. No man may leave his wagon unless he obtains permission from his officer.

From Brigham Young's orders for the journey (Young also divided the Mormons into groups of 100 with a captain in charge)

SOURCE E: THE IMPACT OF YOUNG'S WORK

By 1860 more than 40,000 people were living in Utah. The majority of them were Mormons. By 1865 277 canals provided water for more than 150,000 acres of land.

***The Story of the Great American West*, 1977**

Even when the Mormons arrived at the Great Salt Lake Young did not relax. He decided exactly where they would settle, and it was Young who was responsible for laying out their new city and establishing the farms and industries needed to support the Mormons in their new home.

things **to do**

Task 1:
Look carefully at the sources provided and, using your own knowledge as well, complete the chart below.

Problems	What Young did

Task 2:
Using the information in the sources, and your own knowledge, answer the following question:
How important was Brigham Young in the success of the Mormons' move to the Great Salt Lake?

investigation 4.3 What was the Great Salt Lake like?

SOURCE A

This is the place which the Lord has Chosen for us to commence our settlements.

Brigham Young's comment on first seeing the Great Salt Lake

SOURCE B

▲ *The Mormons' first view of the Great Salt Lake*

SOURCE C

There is an extensive, beautiful, level looking valley from here to the lake. There is little timber anywhere which is about the only objection which could be raised. For my own part I am happily disappointed in the appearance of the valley of the Salt Lake. If the land is as rich as it appears to be I have no doubt that the Saints can live here and do well.

William Clayton, one of the early Mormon settlers

SOURCE D

I could not describe my feelings. Everything looked gloomy and I felt heart sick. Weak and weary as I am, I would rather go a thousand miles farther than remain in such a desolate and forsaken spot as this.

Brigham Young's sister-in-law describes her feelings on seeing the Great Salt Lake

things **to do**

Task 1:
Read Sources A to D, above.
Using the sources, and your own knowledge, answer the following questions:

a How useful is Source A to someone studying the reasons why the Mormons chose to live at the Great Salt Lake?

b Source B is a drawing of the Great Salt Lake. Does that mean it must be unreliable?

c Does Source C support Source B? Explain your answer.

d What reasons does Clayton give in Source C to explain why he is 'happily disappointed' with the area?

e Why do you think the view of the Great Salt Lake given in Source D is so different from that given in the other sources?

investigation 4.4 How well did the Mormons cope at the Great Salt Lake?

The Great Salt Lake had both advantages and disadvantages for the Mormons. The land was flat and appeared fertile. It supported few trees but the mud from the lake side could be shaped and hardened into bricks. There was limited water but the streams could be dammed and the water diverted to irrigate the fields. Within a day of their arrival the Mormons began ploughing and planting their crops.

Although life was hard the Mormons struggled on and, under the leadership of Brigham Young, began building their new city. In the centre were public buildings including a temple and a meeting place. Streets surrounded the central square in neat, organised lines.

In 1850 a US Army engineer called Captain Howard Stansbury visited Salt Lake City and described what he saw:

> A city has been laid out on a magnificent scale. Through the city itself flows an unfailing stream of pure, sweet water which, by an ingenious method of irrigation, is made to go along each side of every street from which it is led into every garden, spreading life and beauty over what was previously a barren waste. The houses are built, principally, of sun-dried brick which makes a warm, comfortable building, giving a very neat appearance.

To make the Mormons fully self-sufficient, industries were started. Mormon silk was produced and flax was grown for weaving. Not all industries were successful, however, the word went out to Mormons everywhere to come to the Salt Lake. A fund was set up to help pay for travel but, when funds ran low, Brigham Young urged the Mormons to build handcarts and walk – they did! Many died, but hundreds more, including some from England and Wales, successfully made the journey.

DESERET

The Mormons originally chose to settle at the Great Salt Lake because the area was:

- isolated from non-Mormon neighbours; and
- part of Mexico and therefore away from American interference.

In 1848 America won a war against Mexico which resulted in the area of the Great Salt Lake being given to America. To protect the Mormons Brigham Young proposed that the area should become an independent Mormon state with their own laws and government. The new state was to be called Deseret.

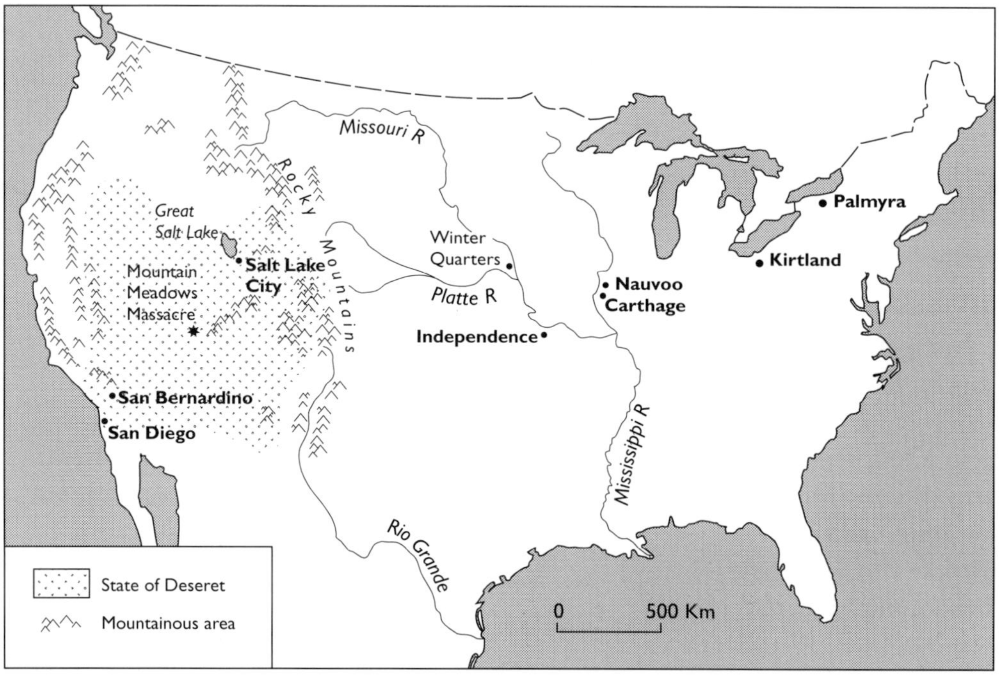

◀ *A map showing the proposed Mormon state of Deseret*

In the east anti-Mormon feeling ran high. The Government responded by refusing the Mormon request. Instead the area became the Territory of Utah with Young as the first Governor. Non-Mormon officials were constantly abused or worse. In 1857 matters came to a head and 1,500 soldiers were sent to Salt Lake City to enforce US laws. The Mormons responded by evacuating their city and fleeing into the hills. After the deaths of 140 pioneers at nearby Mountain Meadows the Government was keen to seek a peaceful solution. The Mormons were persuaded to return to their city and an agreement was reached. The Government made clear that it would not interfere with the Mormon religion but they would have to accept a non-Mormon Governor. Utah would not become a state until the Mormons gave up polygamy, which they did in 1890.

things **to do**

- **Task 1:**
  Using the information provided in this investigation, and your own knowledge, complete the following chart listing the changes made to the area of the Great Salt Lake. One example has been added to help you.

- **Task 2:**
  Use the information from this investigation, and your own knowledge, to produce a flow chart showing the main events, in order, which led to the creation of the state of Utah. Use as many boxes as you need.

Changes made
They dammed the streams and used the water to irrigate the land

issue 5

The cowboys and cattle

the **big** picture

Key Questions

- Who were the cowboys?
- What did the cowboys wear and why?
- Why did the Long Drives begin and who was responsible?
- What was life like for cowboys on the Long Drive?
- How and why did cattle ranching change by 1890?
- Why are the images of the cowboys often so far from reality?

The cowboys have become a symbol of the American West and, over the years, have been portrayed either as 'good' heroes saving the west from the 'bad' Indians, or as cold-blooded gunslingers. Such stereotypes are now accepted as the truth and have become very hard to change.

The idea of the gunfight has become an established part of the western myth. A gunfight always has the opponents starting a long way away from each other; they walk slowly forwards; the fixed stares; the dramatic music and finally the first to draw. A real hero will show his skill, and compassion, by shooting the gun away from his opponent's hand rather than killing him.

And who were these heroes? According to such movies as *High Plains Drifter* and *Pale Rider*, the cowboy has become a loner without a name but lethal with a gun. He is almost invariably white skinned.

The reality is far removed from the movie image . . .

Did you know?

Most cowboys chewed tobacco. When the wad of tobacco had lost its taste it would be spat out into a container on the floor called a spittoon. Such spitting was only considered bad manners if you missed the spittoon!

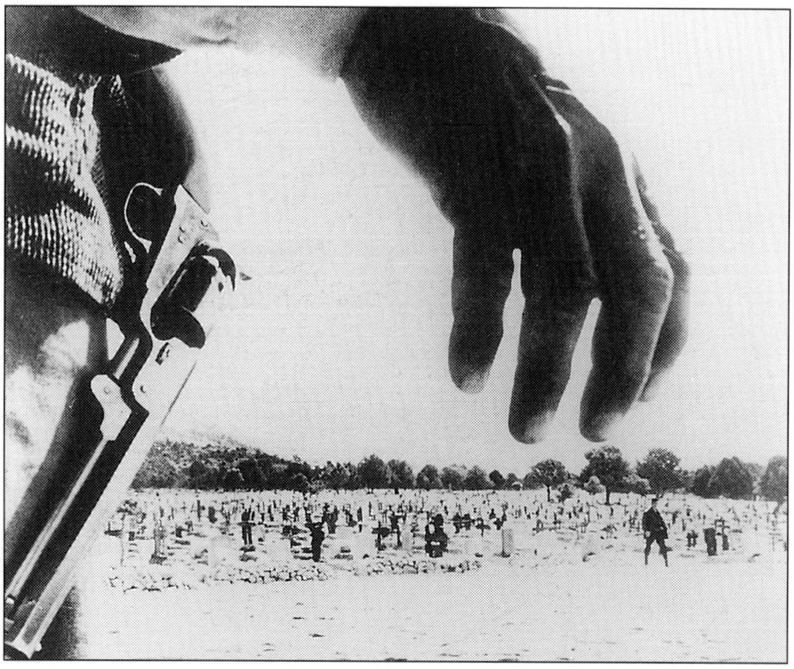

◀ *The gunfight in the cemetery from the film,* The Good, the Bad and the Ugly

investigation 5.1 Who were the cowboys?

SOURCE A

▲ *A Black cowboy*

SOURCE B

Not all cowboys were Anglo-Saxon types as shown by the film-makers. Not unnaturally, a good many of them were negroes. When the cattle drives began 182,000 slaves lived in Texas. Many of them were used to life in the saddle. In fact, around one third of all cowboys were black or Mexican.

Billington and Huntingdon, *Westward Expansion*, 1947

SOURCE C

Most cowboys were Southerners and they were a wild, reckless bunch.

Teddy Blue, a former cowboy

SOURCE D

Some cowboys were rotten. John Hardin was one of them. While driving 1,200 longhorns on the Chisholm Trail to Abilene he shot two Indians. A little further along the trail he got into a row with some Mexican cowherds. He settled that squabble by killing five of them.

R Hassrick, *The American West*, 1975

SOURCE E

His soft hat was pushed back. A loose knotted dull-scarlet handkerchief sagged from his throat and one casual thumb was hooked in the cartridge belt that slanted across his hips.

Owen Wister, *The Virginian*, 1956.

Did you know?

The word cowboy was first used in Ireland over a thousand years ago. It was used in America during the Revolution (1775–83) to describe farmers who sided with the British.

▲ *Mexican vaqueros – before the Civil War most cowboys in Texas were Mexican*

things **to do**

Task 1:

Look at the sources in this investigation and answer the following questions:

a Look at Sources B, C and F. According to them what sorts of people became cowboys?

b Does Source A prove Source B is reliable?

c Does Source C support Source D?

d Source E is from a novel. Does this mean that the description of the cowboy cannot be reliable?

Task 2:

Using the information from the sources, and your own knowledge, answer the following question:

What sorts of people became cowboys?

investigation 5.2 What did the cowboys wear and why?

The cowboy's clothing was designed to be functional and allow him to do his work in relative comfort and safety. The image of the gun-toting cowboy as portrayed in the westerns is rather removed from the truth. For example, most cowboys did not carry a handgun – they were simply too expensive. Shooting a gun near a herd of cattle could easily start a stampede and a number of ranches actually had rules forbidding their employees from carrying guns!

THE COWBOYS' EQUIPMENT

The dress of the cowboy was picturesque and distinctive. It was, however, not worn with the view of producing an effect but rather for comfort and convenience.

The hat was made of felt. The broad brim protected the wearer from the sun and was an umbrella in rainy weather. In winter it could be pulled down over the ears and tied thus giving protection from frostbite. It was used to fan the campfires; swung in the air it was a way of signalling. It might be folded and used as a pillow. These hats were usually called **'stetsons'** after the Philadelphia manufacturer who made them.

The bandana. The handkerchief (usually a red bandana) which was worn around the neck and intended for use as a mask. When the cowboy rode along behind the herd of cattle, he pulled the handkerchief up over his nose and mouth protecting himself from the cloud of alkaline dust.

The 'chaps' were an overgarment like a pair of trousers with a cut-out seat. Many were made of the shaggy skin of a bear, goat or sheep. Should a horse fall on a man, the fur-faced 'chaps' would protect his leg. They were also able to withstand the thorny vegetation. They kept the rider's legs from becoming chafed during a long ride and protected him from the cutting north wind in winter.

Coat, vest and gloves. The cowboy liked to go coatless whenever possible, but he always wore a vest (waistcoat). This was usually left unbuttoned. In cold weather and while roping, gloves were usually worn.

Boots and spurs. All cowboys wore high-heeled boots. The heel and arch were so constructed that the foot and leg were comfortable when riding. Spurs were worn at all times.

Saddle. The saddle was the cowboy's throne – its bumps and contours grew to fit the owner's body. A man might gamble away his money, horse or chaps, but he would put his saddle on his back and return home on foot.

▲ *This description has been taken from 'The Long Drive' by Dick Everett which appeared in* Collections of The Kansas State Historical Society 1926–8

things **to do**

Task 1:
Using the photograph of a cowboy below, label and describe the purpose of each piece of equipment carried by the cowboy.

Did you know?

Although cowboy spurs look dangerous they were actually used very carefully – spur marks on a horse were a sign of poor horsemanship.

Felt hat (stetson) used to . . .

investigation 5.3 Why did the Long Drives begin and who was responsible?

The **Long Drives** were very aptly named. They involved driving cattle (often more than 1,500 at a time) from the ranches of Texas to the nearest railroad stations over 1,000 miles away – hence the name.

The first cattle ranches originated in Texas on the southern Plains. Here, Mexican vaqueros allowed the cattle to roam free on the open grasslands identifying their own cattle by means of a system of branching (burning a design into the hide of a cow with a red hot poker). When Texas became independent in 1836 the Mexicans left, abandoning their land which was taken over by American settlers. The new owners of the Texas plains inherited a thriving tradition of cattle ranching, which they preserved, largely unaltered. That explains why so many words associated with cowboys sound Spanish. Some examples are given below:

- **Bronco:** Spanish for 'wild' or 'rough'. Given to any wild horse.
- **Chaparejos:** Mexican Spanish for 'leggings worn as protection against cactus or thorny bushes'.
- **Cinch:** from the Spanish *cincha* – a wide strap with rings at the end which passes under a horse's belly and holds the saddle on.
- **Lariat:** from the Spanish *la reata*, meaning rope.
- **Lasso:** Spanish for a 'noose'.
- **Pinto:** Spanish for 'painted' and used to describe spotted horses.
- **Ranch:** From the Spanish *rancho*.

In 1861 the American Civil War began and many Texas cattlemen joined the Southern (or Confederate) armies, often serving far from their home state.

▲ *Soldiers of the 1st Texas Brigade (Confederate States Army) outside their winter camp near Quantico, Virginia, in 1861. Any Texans like these men served a long way away from their homes*

The Civil War raged on for four years and cost the lives of over 600,000 men – it was America's bloodiest war. The South was devastated by the war but the cattle, abandoned on the Plains by their owners, had thrived. By 1865 there were estimated to have been over five million cattle on the Plains. Over the years the cattle had become leaner but much hardier and were now able to withstand most weather conditions. Indeed, there were so many cattle on the plains that they had become almost worthless. In the northern states cattle were scarce and were fetching over ten times their value in Texas. The potential for vast profits was obvious. The problem was how to get the cattle from Texas to the northern markets. The solution was the Long Drive!

To prepare for the Long Drive cowboys needed to round up, or gather in, the cattle from the Plains. This was not an easy job. Despite line camps being established around the herd throughout the winter to prevent wandering, the cattle were still scattered over a large area. As the ground thawed in the spring many cattle became bogged down in the mud near water holes. These cattle needed to be roped and pulled clear – known as bog-riding. Once the cattle had been rounded up the brands needed to be inspected. Any cattle with another rancher's brand needed to be cut out and returned to their owner. Young animals still unbranded then needed to be roped and branded with the ranch or trail brands. Finally, the herd could be fattened ready for the long drive north.

The success of the Long Drives owed much to the efforts of three men:

JOSEPH MCCOY

Joseph McCoy was a cattle trader in Chicago, Illinois. He saw that by providing a centre for collecting cattle near a railhead he could control the flow of cattle to the east and make a good profit! He chose to build the first 'cow town' at Abilene, Kansas, in 1867. His reputation for honesty led to the phrase 'the real McCoy'.

CHARLES GOODNIGHT

Charles Goodnight returned from the Civil War to find that his cattle had dramatically increased in number. In 1860 his herd had numbered just 180 cows but by 1865 it had increased to 5,000. He decided to sell his cattle to the Government to feed Indians on the newly established reservations. In partnership with Oliver Loving he created the famous Goodnight–Loving trail.

JESSE CHISHOLM

During the American Civil War Jesse Chisholm, a half-Cherokee trader, planned to trade with the Indian tribes along the Washita. A cattle herder moving his cattle north from Texas came across Chisholm's trail and followed it through to Kansas. Chisholm's work with the Indians did much to avoid trouble.

Did you know?

When cattle trails crossed Indian land the cowboys were usually charged a dollar per head of cattle. Many cattlemen employed Indians to help negotiate the fee.

Did you know?

Some people made huge fortunes from cattle. Charles Goodnight owned and leased over half a million hectares (1.25 million acres) of land in Texas.

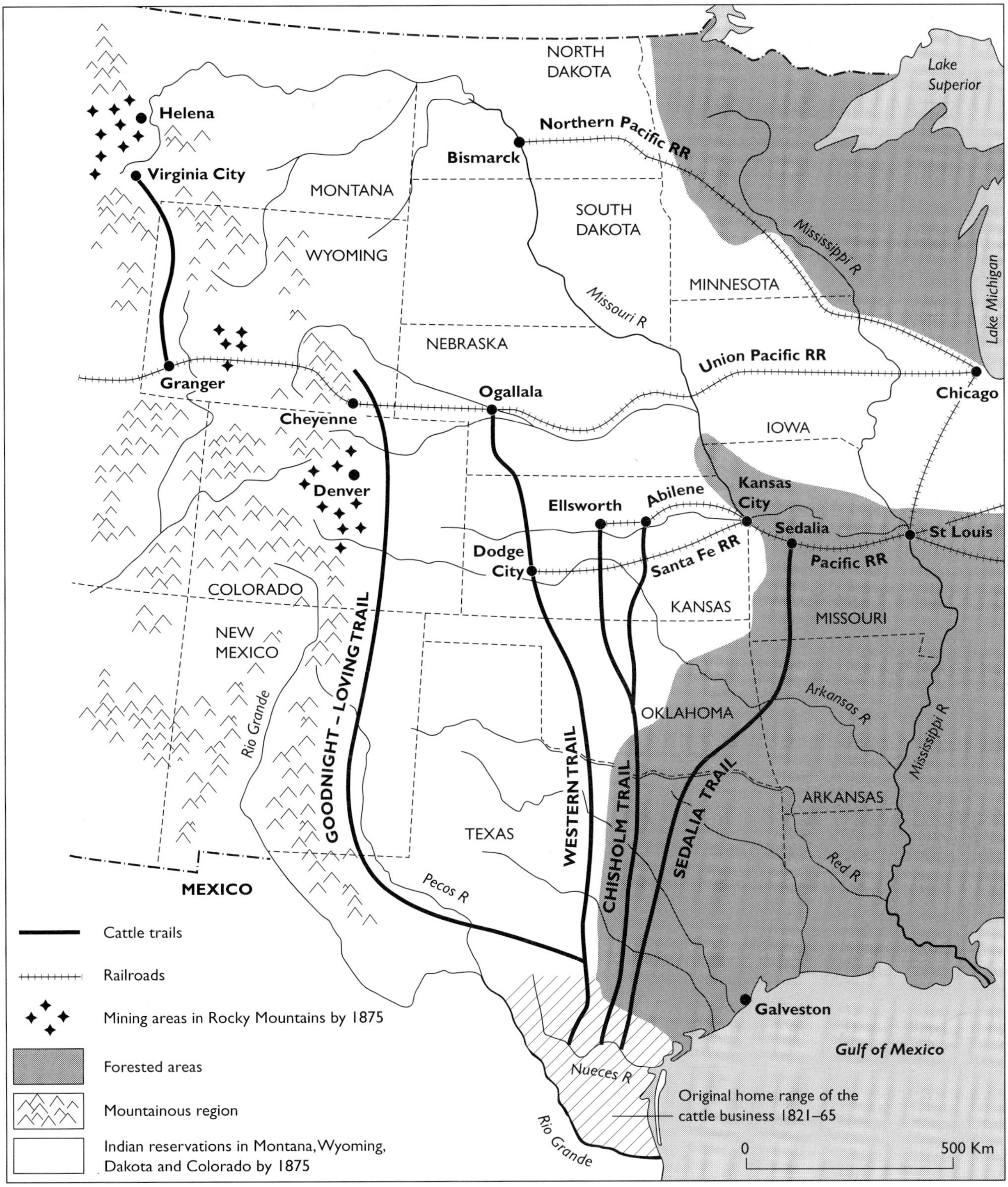

▲ *Cattle trails in the American West*

Eventually the cattlemen began to realise that it made sense to graze cattle on the northern Plains – nearer to the railroad stations. One of the first men to grasp this idea was John Iliff who built up a flourishing business selling cattle to the Indian reservations and railroad companies.

In 1881 a journalist by the name of James Brisbin published a book entitled *The Beef Bonanza* or *How to get rich on the Plains*. This book attracted hundreds of people to the Plains, convinced that they would return rich beyond belief. Even British aristocrats, French counts and German barons were caught up in 'the beef bonanza'.

things **to do**

- **Task 1:**
  Read the information provided in this investigation about the background to the Long Drives.

  Use the boxes below to explain the events which led to the Long Drives (one box has already been completed to help you). Add more boxes if you need them.

- **Task 2:**
  Using the information in this investigation, and your own knowledge, answer the following question:
  How important was the Civil War (1861–5) in building up the cattle industry in the west?
  Explain your answer.

FLOW DIAGRAM TO SHOW THE CAUSES OF THE LONG DRIVE:

1 Americans took over the Mexican cattle trade after Texas became an Independent state.

2

3

4

5

6

investigation 5.4 What was life like for cowboys on the Long Drive?

The activities in this investigation focus on a game which will need to be prepared before the investigation begins. The cards on the following pages need to be cut out and the gameboard assembled.

things **to do**

- **Task 1:**

CATTLE TRAILS BOARD GAME

RULES OF THE GAME

The game can be played by up to *four* teams.
A team should consist of two players – one to collect cards and one to follow the instructions.

HOW TO PLAY

Place the five sets of cards *face down* in the box on the board.

Teams should decide who goes first by throwing the dice.

One player from the first team collects a **round-up** card from the pack and reads it out. Any instructions should be followed and the card kept. Each team should hold onto all cards they pick up in the order collected.

When the first team have had their go a player from the next team picks up the next card in the **round-up** stack.

This pattern is repeated until a card is found giving an instruction to start on a particular trail. From that point on the team will collect cards from the appropriate **trail** pack and *not* the **round-up** pack. Once every team has started up a trail the race is on to see who will be the quickest to complete the journey to the cow towns.

things **to do**

- **Task 2:**
  When you have finished task 1 each team should use the information from their cards to create a journal which will record their experiences on the Long Drive.

JOURNAL

The round-up:

Day 1 ....

Day 2 ....

Day 3 ....

Day 4 ....

Day 5 ....

Day 6 ....

Day 7 ....

The Long Drive:

Day 1 ....

Day 2 ....

Day 3 ....

Day 4 ....

Day 5 ....

Day 6 ....

Day 7 ....

Day 8 ....

Day 9 ....

Day 10 ....

Day 11 ....

Day 12 ....

Day 13 ....

Day 14 ....

Day 15 ....

Day 16 ....

Day 17 ....

Day 18 ....

Day 19 ....

Day 20 ....

Arrival:

Your cattle are counted. A price is agreed depending on the number and their condition. The cowboys are paid off and return home.

- **Task 3:**
  Using the information from your journal, and your own knowledge, answer the following question:
  What was life like for the cowboys on the Long Drive?

ROUND-UP CARDS

You have enough cattle. You decide to head along the **GOODNIGHT–LOVING TRAIL** towards Cheyenne. **COLLECT THE *G-L TRAIL* PACK**	You have enough cattle. You decide to head along the **WESTERN TRAIL** towards Ogallala. **COLLECT THE *WESTERN TRAIL* PACK**
You have enough cattle. You decide to head along the **CHISHOLM TRAIL** towards Abilene or Ellsworth. **COLLECT THE *CHISHOLM TRAIL* PACK**	You have enough cattle. You decide to head along the **SEDALIA TRAIL** towards Sedalia. **COLLECT THE *SEDALIA TRAIL* PACK**
Heavy rain delays your start. **MISS A GO**	You are able to recruit an experienced team of cowboys ahead of your rivals. **HAVE ANOTHER GO**
Good weather allows you to make good progress. Your round-up is nearly complete. **HAVE ANOTHER GO**	Your cowboys are all out on the range locating cattle. Nothing to report.
You round-up 2,500 'mossy-horn' cattle from woods south of the Nueces River but they are wild and need to be carefully watched.	Heavy rain and melting snow have led to many cattle becoming trapped near water supplies. These take time to recover. **MISS A GO**
Your round-up is going well. You bring in a large number of young, unbranded calves and mavericks. **HAVE ANOTHER GO**	You hear that the price of cattle in the northern markets has now gone up to $28 a head! **HAVE ANOTHER GO**
Your cowboys are all out on the range collecting cattle. Nothing to report.	Some of your cowboys are found drunk and are fired. You need to hire more. **MISS A GO**
Your round-up is going well. The cattle are being brought in and the branding is under way.	You are gathering together the supplies and remuda (group of spare horses) needed for the Long Drive. Coming along well.
The cattle have scattered over a large area. You will need more time to round-up than originally planned. **MISS A GO**	You are pulling together a herd of some 2,500 animals. You have a large number of cattle brought in with confusing brands and hire a brand reader to help. This takes time.

Cattle trails board game

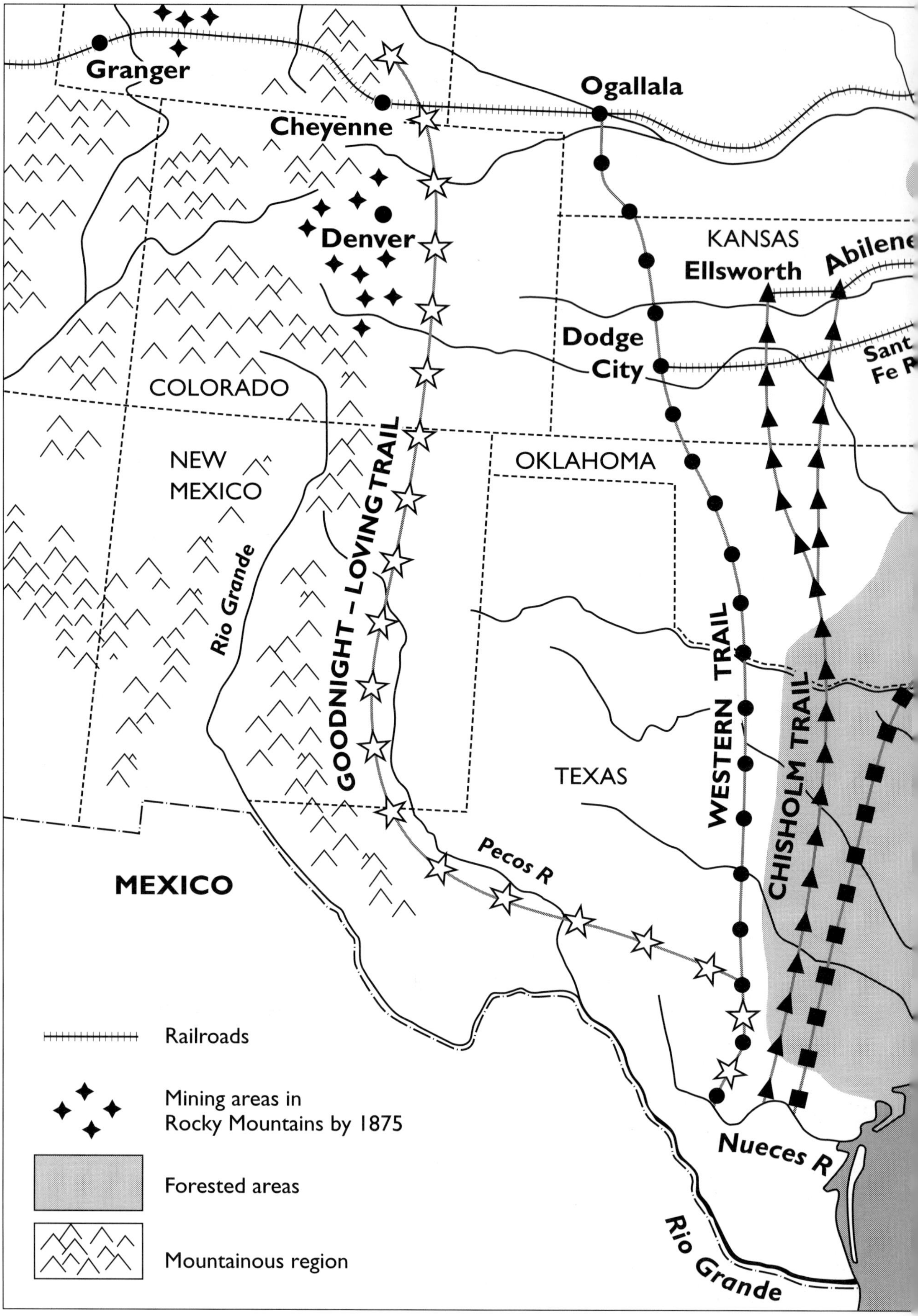

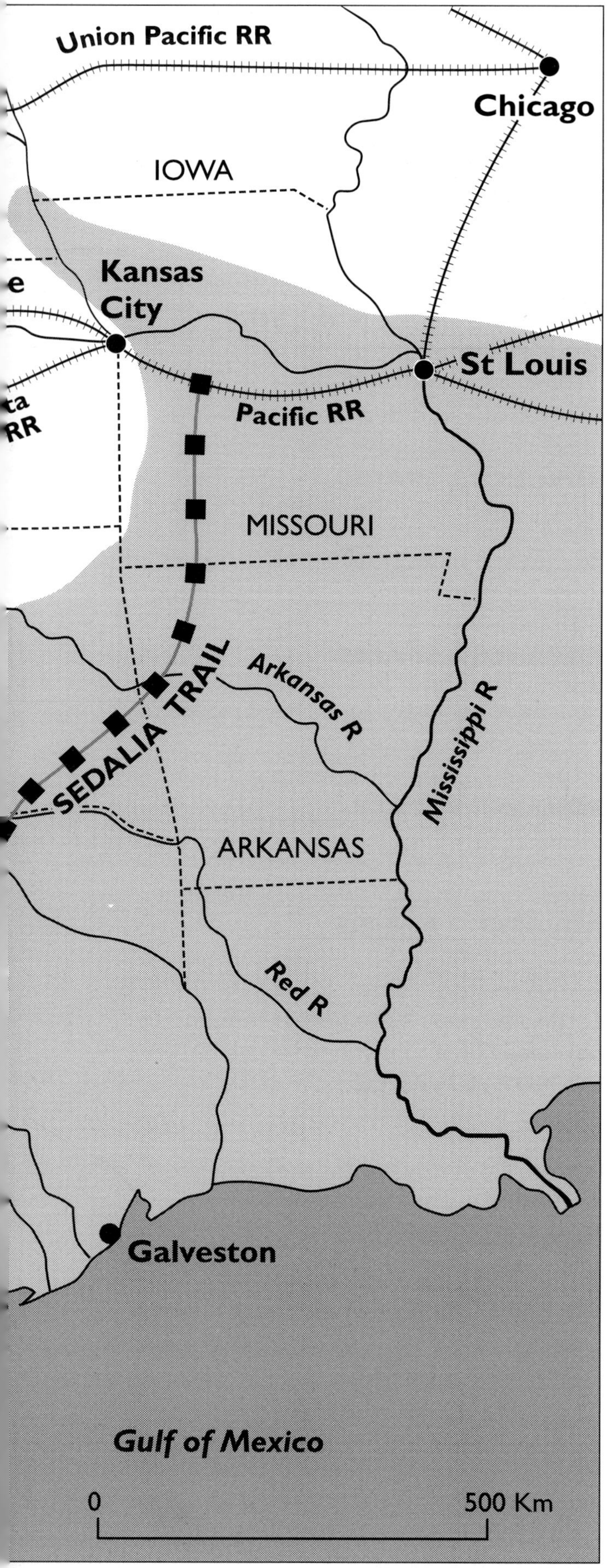

ROUND-UP CARDS

CHISHOLM TRAIL PACK ▲

SEDALIA TRAIL PACK ■

GOODNIGHT–LOVING TRAIL PACK ☆

WESTERN TRAIL PACK ●

CHISHOLM TRAIL PACK

Another herd follows you along the trail but you have a good start. **ADVANCE 4 SPACES**	Cattle stampede – the herd is contained but needs time to rest and recover. **DO NOT ADVANCE**
You approach a river late in the day and decide to rest the herd until the next morning. **DO NOT ADVANCE**	Cattle stampede – the herd is not contained. 180 animals killed or lost. Time spent gathering and resting herd. **MISS A GO**
You are told of a short cut which could cut two days off your journey. **ADVANCE 4 SPACES**	The trail ahead is clear and the weather is good. **ADVANCE 3 SPACES**
Strong winds create a dust storm and make progress difficult. **ADVANCE 1 SPACE**	You meet Indians. They agree to accept three cattle in return for passage through their lands. **ADVANCE 2 SPACES**
You meet hostile Indians. You gather the herd together and mount extra guards at night until the threat has passed. **DO NOT ADVANCE**	You meet homesteaders. They prepare to oppose your passage through their settlements. You re-route around them. **ADVANCE 1 SPACE**
The crossing of an unusually fast river costs the lives of two men. You stop to bury them. **DO NOT ADVANCE**	The chuck wagon loses a wheel. You pause to replace it. The job is soon done. **ADVANCE 2 SPACES**
The trail ahead is clear and the weather is good. **ADVANCE 3 SPACES**	Cattle stampede – the herd is contained but needs time to rest and recover. **DO NOT ADVANCE**
The trail ahead is clear and the weather is good. **ADVANCE 3 SPACES**	Despite storms overnight the cattle are kept calm and a stampede is avoided. **ADVANCE 2 SPACES**
The cattle are blinded by the sun on the approach to a river crossing. They will not cross until the sun has moved around. **ADVANCE 1 SPACE**	The trail ahead is clear and the weather is good. **ADVANCE 3 SPACES**
The price of cattle on the eastern market has fallen. This means less profit. **DO NOT ADVANCE**	A number of cattle traders are in Abilene and Ellsworth and are keen to trade. This means higher prices and more profit. **ADVANCE 2 SPACES**

SEDALIA TRAIL PACK

The Arkansas River (often the most dangerous part of this trail) is low. There has been little rain.
ADVANCE 4 SPACES

Cattle stampede – the herd is contained but needs time to rest and recover.
DO NOT ADVANCE

You approach a river late in the day – you rest the cattle until next morning.
DO NOT ADVANCE

Cattle stampede – the herd is not contained. 180 animals killed or lost. Time spent gathering and resting herd.
MISS A GO

You are told of a short cut which could cut two days off your journey.
ADVANCE 4 SPACES

The trail ahead is clear and the weather is good.
ADVANCE 3 SPACES

Strong winds create a dust storm which makes progress difficult.
ADVANCE 1 SPACE

You meet Indians. They agree to accept three cattle in return for passage through their lands.
ADVANCE 2 SPACES

You meet hostile Indians. You gather the herd together and mount extra guards at night until the threat has passed.
DO NOT ADVANCE

You meet homesteaders. They prepare to oppose your passage through their settlements. You re-route around them.
ADVANCE 1 SPACE

The crossing of an unusually fast river costs the lives of two men. You stop to bury them.
DO NOT ADVANCE

The chuck wagon loses a wheel. You pause to replace it. The job is soon done.
ADVANCE 2 SPACES

The trail ahead is clear and the weather is good.
ADVANCE 3 SPACES

Cattle stampede – the herd is contained but needs time to rest and recover.
DO NOT ADVANCE

The trail ahead is clear and the weather is good.
ADVANCE 3 SPACES

Despite storms overnight the cattle are kept calm and a stampede is avoided.
ADVANCE 2 SPACES

Sun blinds the cattle on the approach to a river crossing and they will not cross until the sun moves around.
ADVANCE 1 SPACE

The trail ahead is clear and the weather is good.
ADVANCE 3 SPACES

The price of cattle on the eastern market has fallen. This means less profit.
DO NOT ADVANCE

A number of cattle traders are in Sedalia and are keen to trade. This will keep the price high so more profit can be made.
ADVANCE 2 SPACES

GOODNIGHT–LOVING TRAIL PACK

Part of your herd is bought by agents of the Bureau of Indian Affairs to feed the reservation Indians.
ADVANCE 4 SPACES

Cattle stampede – the herd is contained but needs time to rest and recover.
DO NOT ADVANCE

You approach a river late in the day. You rest the cattle until next morning.
DO NOT ADVANCE

Cattle stampede – the herd is not contained. 180 animals killed or lost. Time spent gathering and resting herd.
MISS A GO

You are told of a short cut which could cut two days off your journey.
ADVANCE 4 SPACES

The trail ahead is clear and the weather is good.
ADVANCE 3 SPACES

Strong winds create a dust storm which makes progress difficult.
ADVANCE 1 SPACE

You meet Indians. They agree to accept three cattle in return for passage through their lands.
ADVANCE 2 SPACES

You meet hostile Indians. You gather the herd together and mount extra guards at night until the threat passes.
DO NOT ADVANCE

You meet homesteaders. They prepare to oppose your passage through their settlements. You re-route around them.
ADVANCE 1 SPACE

The crossing of an unusually fast river costs the lives of two men. You stop to bury them.
DO NOT ADVANCE

The chuck wagon loses a wheel. You pause to replace it. The job is soon done.
ADVANCE 2 SPACES

The trail ahead is clear and the weather is good.
ADVANCE 3 SPACES

Cattle stampede – the herd is contained but needs time to rest and recover.
DO NOT ADVANCE

The trail ahead is clear and the weather is good.
ADVANCE 3 SPACES

Despite storms overnight the cattle are kept calm and a stampede is avoided.
ADVANCE 2 SPACES

The cattle are blinded by the sun on the approach to a river crossing. They will not cross until the sun moves around.
ADVANCE 1 SPACE

The trail ahead is clear and the weather is good.
ADVANCE 3 SPACES

The price of cattle on the eastern market has fallen. This means less profit.
DO NOT ADVANCE

A number of cattle traders are in Cheyenne and are keen to trade. This will keep prices high and means more profit.
ADVANCE 2 SPACES

WESTERN TRAIL PACK

Cowboys stop off at Dodge City for refreshments and to restock on supplies. Everyone is well rested. **ADVANCE 4 SPACES**	Cattle stampede – the herd is contained but needs time to rest and recover. **DO NOT ADVANCE**
You approach a river late in the day and decide to rest the herd until the next morning. **DO NOT ADVANCE**	Cattle stampede – the herd is not contained. 180 animals killed or lost. Time spent gathering and resting herd. **MISS A GO**
You are told of a short cut which could cut two days off your journey. **ADVANCE 4 SPACES**	The trail ahead is clear and the weather is good. **ADVANCE 3 SPACES**
Strong winds create a dust storm which makes progress difficult. **ADVANCE 1 SPACE**	You meet Indians. They agree to accept three cattle in return for passage through their lands. **ADVANCE 2 SPACES**
You meet hostile Indians. You gather the herd together and mount extra guards at night until the threat has passed. **DO NOT ADVANCE**	You meet homesteaders. They prepare to oppose your passage through their settlements. You re-route around them. **ADVANCE 1 SPACE**
The crossing of an unusually fast river costs the lives of two men. You stop to bury them. **DO NOT ADVANCE**	The chuck wagon loses a wheel. You pause to replace it. The job is soon done. **ADVANCE 2 SPACES**
The trail ahead is clear and the weather is good. **ADVANCE 3 SPACES**	Cattle stampede – the herd is contained but needs time to rest and recover. **DO NOT ADVANCE**
The trail ahead is clear and the weather is good. **ADVANCE 3 SPACES**	Despite storms overnight the cattle are kept calm and a stampede is avoided. **ADVANCE 2 SPACES**
The cattle are blinded by the sun on the approach to a river. They will not cross until the sun has moved around. **ADVANCE 1 SPACE**	The trail ahead is clear and the weather is good. **ADVANCE 3 SPACES**
The price of cattle on the eastern market has fallen. This means less profit. **DO NOT ADVANCE**	A number of cattle traders are in Ogallala and are keen to trade. This will keep prices high and means more profit. **ADVANCE 2 SPACES**

investigation 5.5 How and why did cattle ranching change by 1890?

The work of John Iliff and the popularity of Brisbin's book *How to get rich on the Plains* brought floods of people onto the Plains convinced that all they had to do was buy cattle and leave them to graze for a while in order to make a vast profit. For a while this appeared to be true, but things were soon to change.

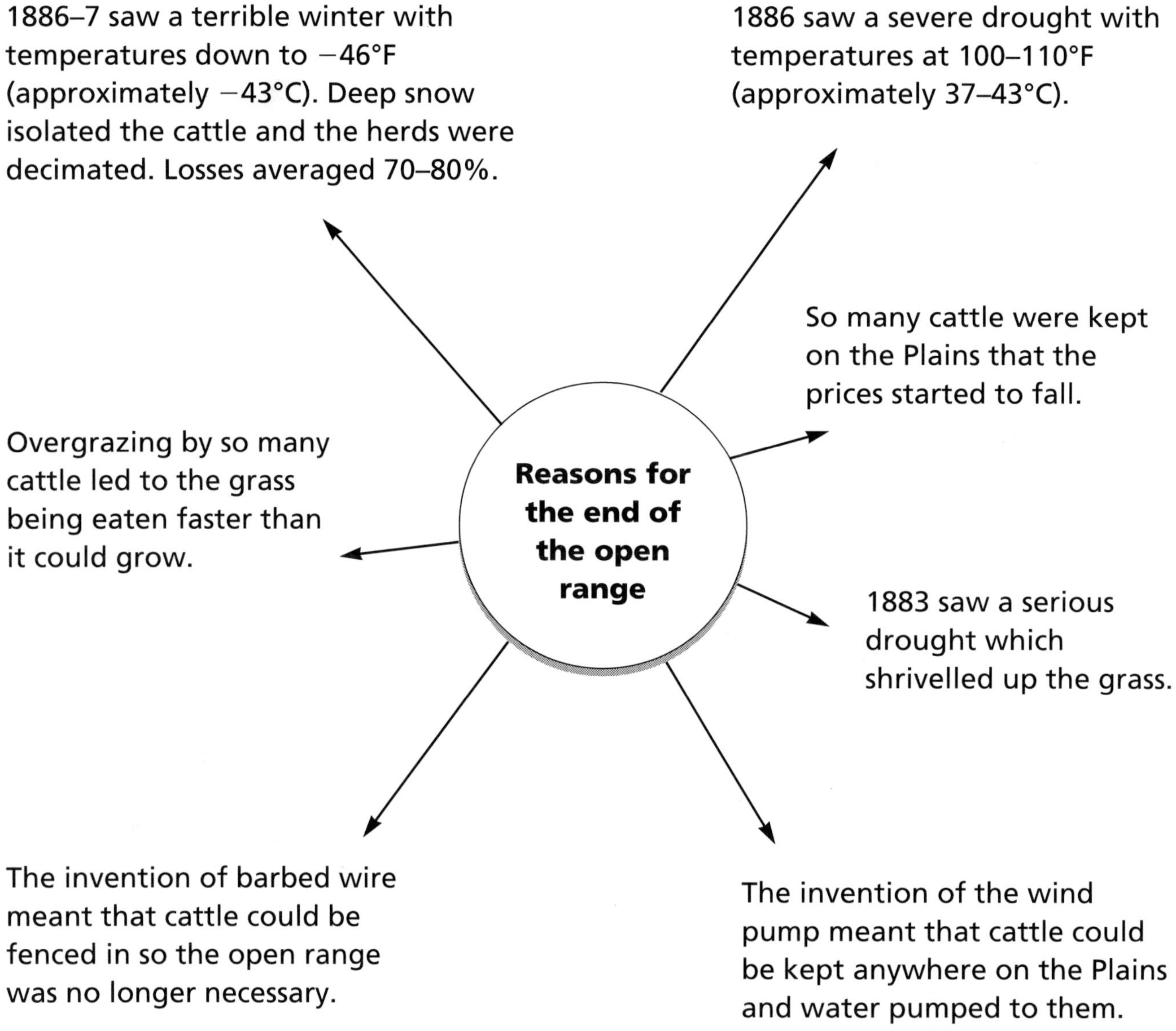

Did you know?

The first refrigerated cattle truck was invented by Gustavus Swift in 1881. This meant that cattle could be slaughtered anywhere and the carcasses shipped east by rail.

things **to do**

- **Task 1:**
  Which of the causes (if any) of the end of the open range do you think was the most important? **Explain your answer.**

- **Task 2:**
  Look carefully at the picture below.

▲ The Last of the 5,000 – *a sketch sent by Charles Russell in 1887 in answer to an enquiry about the condition of a herd*

Using the information in this investigation, and your own knowledge, answer the following question:

Explain why the events shown in the picture happened.

things **to do**

- **Task 3:**
  Look carefully at the picture below.

▲ *From a painting called* Riding the Line of the Wire Fence *by Frederick Remington*

Using the picture, and your own knowledge, answer the following question:
Explain how and why the cowboys' job had changed by 1890.

Did you know?

According to Hollywood, cowboys and Indians always fought but, in reality, some Indians became cowboys and many cowboys came to depend on Indian traders for food and other supplies.

investigation 5.6 Why are the images of the cowboys often so far from reality?

The cowboys of the old west were hard-working young men (the average age of the cowboys was 24) doing a dangerous and physically demanding job. There were probably never more than 15,000 cowboys riding the cattle trails. The 'Long Drives' (taking the cattle to the nearest railroad depots) began in 1865 and had ended by 1885 – a period of no more than 20 years. Despite this, the cowboy has become a symbol of the American West.

Even today no charity event would be complete without a 'western show' as the picture below (taken at a charity event in the West Country) shows.

When and why did this image of the cowboy develop? One reason was the apparent glamour of the job. Cowboys often sent studio photographs of themselves to their families back east. The clothes they wore in these photos were designed to look impressive, and were not necessarily accurate. Cowboys were also often known by unusual nicknames like Deadwood Dick, Texas Jack, Buffalo Bill and Wild Bill which further added to the mystique.

People in the eastern cities working nine to five in dull, routine jobs found the image of the cowboy attractive. The image was further reinforced by ex-buffalo hunter Buffalo Bill Cody who, in 1883, assembled a team of skilled cowboys and 'tame' Indians and went on tour in the east under the name Buffalo Bill's Wild West Show. Even the great Sioux chief Sitting Bull was persuaded to work for Buffalo Bill. Buffalo Bill's Wild West Show even travelled to Europe and performed before an enthusiastic Queen Victoria. This was not the only Wild West show however – there were also Tiger Bill's Wild West, Tompkins' Real Wild West (and frontier exhibition), Buffalo Ranch Real Wild West, and Colonel Tim McCoy's Real Wild West to name but a few!

The last train robbery by the Wild Bunch occurred in 1901. By 1903 the first silent movie had been produced glamorising the event and cementing the image of 'the Wild West'.

Finally 'dime novels' (named according to

▲ *Members of a western group called the 'Wyoming Wildbunch' raising money for the charity CLIC (Cancer and Leukaemia in Children). The group provides a variety of western shows*

their price) were extremely popular in the east. The authors (many of whom had never seen the west) either completely invented characters and events or else simply expanded on the truth. Only recently with movies like *Dances With Wolves* has an attempt been made to redress the balance.

Did you know?

As the demand for cattle declined in the last years of the nineteenth century many ranchers began to introduce sheep onto the Plains instead. There were many conflicts between sheep- and cattle-ranchers.

Did you know?

The Colt .45 handgun was actually too heavy to draw quickly. It had a powerful 'kick' which could throw the gun from someone's hand if it was not tightly held. It was also only accurate over a few metres.

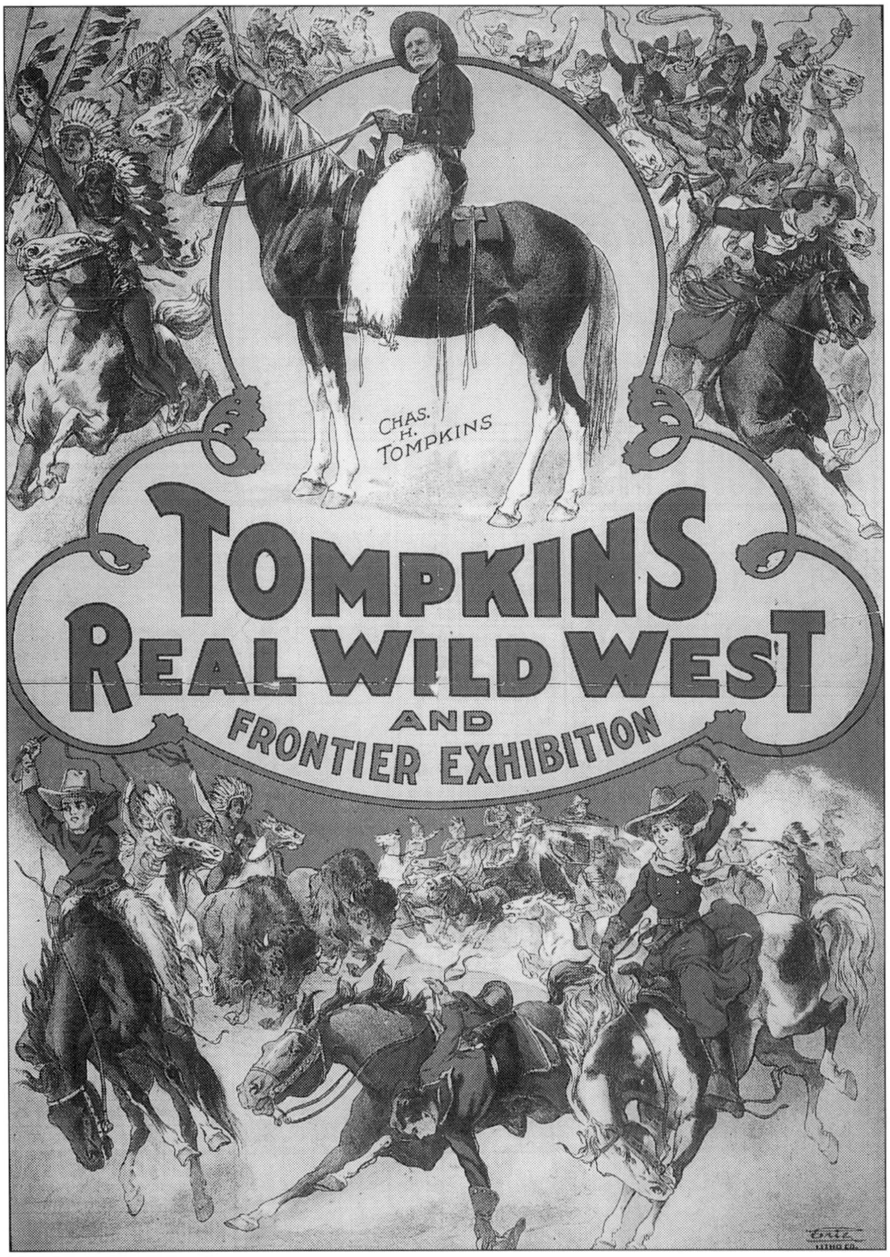

◀ *An advertisement for 'Tompkins' Real Wild West'*

things **to do**

Task 1:

Read the information provided in this investigation which explains why the myth of the 'Wild West' was created. List the reasons given in the space below.

Reasons

Task 2:

Look carefully at the reasons you identified in your list and try to decide which were the most important and why. Put numbers against the reasons in the order of importance – 1 will be the most important, 2 the next and so on.

When you have finished compare your answers with someone else in your class. Try to agree on an order between you. You will need to explain your decisions.

issue 6

The homesteaders

the **big** picture

Key Questions

- Who were the homesteaders and why did they come to the Plains?
- How did the homesteaders survive on the Plains?
- What was life like for women on the Plains?
- What problems did the homesteaders face and how did they deal with them?
- How important were women on the Plains?

The homesteaders were the first group of people to settle on the Plains with the intention of changing the land from grasslands to farmland.

The Mormons and miners only wanted to cross the Plains to settle on lands on the other side. The cattlemen wanted to use the natural resources of the Plains (especially the grass and wide open spaces) to graze their cattle. The homesteaders wanted to change the Plains physically.

As the demand for land on the Plains increased, so more and more land was opened up for settlement. In 1850 the land to the west of Missouri, Arkansas and Iowa was still regarded as Indian land. This land was opened up between 1854 and 1865. After the American Civil War (1861–5) the drier areas of the Plains became settled.

New lands were to be settled according to a pattern devised in the 1780s. All land 'liberated' from the Indians became known as public domain and was owned by the US Government. The new land was surveyed and divided up into a series of ranges. Each range was six miles deep and ran from north to south across the whole of the US. Once surveyed the land was further divided into townships 36 miles square. Some townships were sold complete but others were divided into sections. Each section was one sixth of a township. In each township the Government retained four sections and another was put aside for schools. The rest was put up for sale by auction at a minimum price (originally at 1$ an acre). Few families could afford a whole township and so property speculators bought up much of the land. It soon became apparent that much of the land was not as fertile as had been hoped and many families were unable to survive on their land. To avoid such hardships the Government introduced the Homestead Act in 1862 which promised homesteaders 160 acres of land free, on condition that they lived and worked on the land for at least five years.

Many who came to the Plains were bitterly disappointed with what they found – they had been led to expect a paradise for the taking. Many homesteaders did eventually succeed in establishing a life on the Plains but it was to be a long, hard struggle.

There was certainly no shortage of people looking to move to the Plains. The crush to register new claims at Government Land Offices on newly opened land had to be seen to be believed. In the 1880s officials at Garden City, Kansas entered their offices by means of a ladder at the rear of the building to avoid the crowds.

Between 1870 and 1890, more American land was settled and cultivated than in the previous 250 years of White settlement! 430 million acres of land were claimed and of those, 225 million acres were actually cultivated.

Did you know?

In addition to the weather and environmental hazards, settlers on the Plains also had to deal with tarantula spiders, deadly scorpions and snakes. Even their cows were a potential hazard – cattle rubbing themselves against the fragile soddies or frame houses could cause them to collapse!

By 1890 the Director of the US Government census could report:

> The unsettled area has been so broken into by isolated bodies of settlement that there can hardly be said to be a frontier line.

Although the homesteaders arrived on the Plains with promises of free land and other inducements they often found that the best areas (by rivers or railroads) had already been claimed by the state, railroads or property speculators. The state, railroads and speculators owned a massive half a billion acres by 1890 compared to 80 million owned by homesteaders.

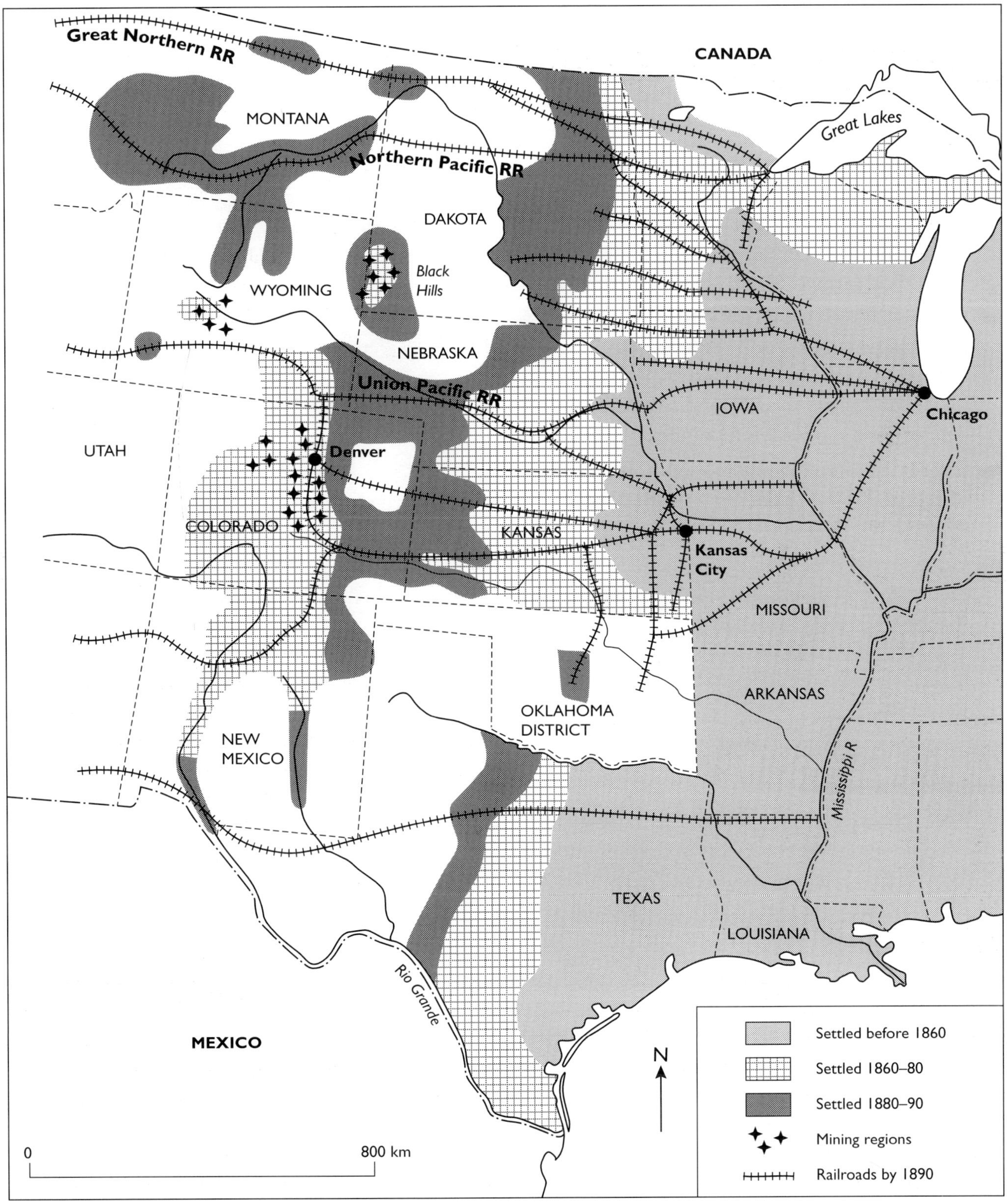

▲ *The map above shows where the new areas of settlement were concentrated*

investigation 6.1 Who were the homesteaders and why did they come to the Plains?

Homesteaders is a broad term which embraces many different people whose single purpose was to establish a new life as farmers on the Plains.

WHERE DID THEY COME FROM?

The people who came to the Great Plains came from many different places:

- By 1880 some 25,000 Blacks had settled in Kansas. Nicodemus was an early Black settlement which became a busy market centre until the railroad passed it by. By 1900 Blacks had farmed 50,000 acres in Nebraska.
- Nearly 400,000 Canadians settled on the Plains between 1880 and 1883. Because of a very good exchange rate with the US dollar they could afford to settle and live reasonably comfortably – at least for a while.
- Over one million people moved from Missouri, Iowa and the other north-western states in the 1880s alone.
- Huge numbers of immigrants came to the Plains from England, Ireland, Scandinavia, Russia and other European countries. The rate of immigration into the United States rose from 500,000 in the 1830s to 5.25 million by the 1880s.

WHY DID THEY COME TO THE PLAINS?

We have already considered many of the reasons why people settled on the Plains in investigation 3.1 (Why did people move onto the Plains?). By the 1870s there were other factors as well and these can be divided into three groups: Government encouragement, the railroads and propaganda.

GOVERNMENT ENCOURAGEMENT

The Homestead Act of 1862 granted settlers 160 acres of land free if they lived and worked on the land for a period of five years. The Timber and Culture Act of 1873 gave the settlers a further 160 acres of land on condition that a certain percentage was planted with trees.

RAILROADS

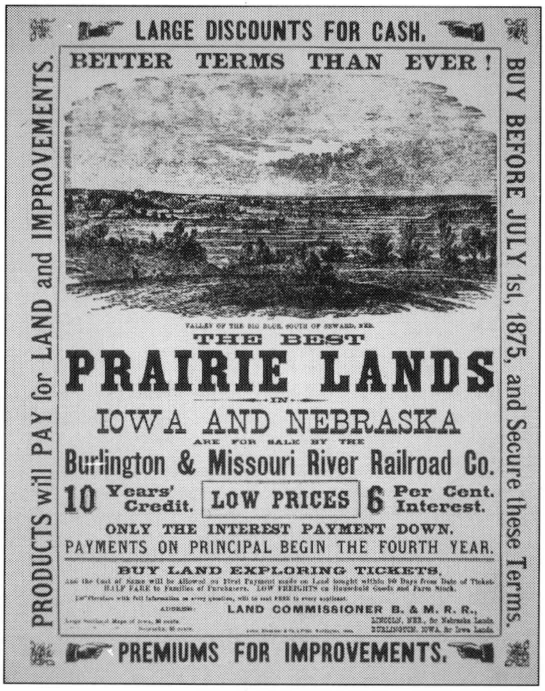

▲ *Large amounts of surplus land owned by the railroad companies were sold to build towns and establish farms*

PROPAGANDA

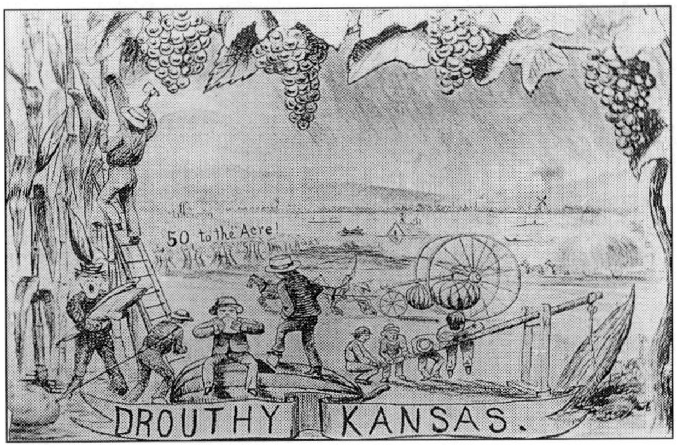

▲ *A poster advertising the attractions of a 'Droughty' Kansas*

It is a good country for corn you ask? Stranger, you will never know what corn country is until you go to Kansas. When the husking is done in the fall the men go out with mallets and wedges and split up the corn stalks for shipment to the east as telegraph poles.

Coolidge Border Ruffian, 10 July 1886

WHAT WERE THE REASONS FOR SUCH ENCOURAGEMENT?

Government encouragement was given as an easy way to complete the policy of manifest destiny and subdue the Indians once and for all.

Propaganda was put out by people already living on the Plains to encourage more people to join them. This would provide more labour and, once the population reached 60,000, the people could apply to become a state. This would give them much more control over their own affairs.

Railroads were out to make money. By selling off their surplus land they could encourage the growth of new settlements. They could then profit by transporting new settlers to these towns. Once the towns became established the railroads could keep them supplied with goods from the east – again at a profit.

things **to do**

Task 1:
Using the information in this investigation and your answers to the tasks in investigation 3.1 (Why did people move onto the Plains?), answer the following question:
What sort of people were the homesteaders?

Task 2:
Use the information on the previous pages, and your own knowledge, to answer the following question:
The railroads were the most important factor in encouraging homesteaders onto the Plains.
Do you agree? Explain your answer.

▲ *A Nebraska couple pose outside their sod-house*

investigation 6.2 How did the homesteaders survive on the Plains?

One of the biggest problems on the Plains was simply providing shelter. The harsh conditions tolerated few trees and so building materials were scarce. In desperation the homesteaders used the soil itself to build houses known as sod houses or 'soddies'.

Sod-houses came in a large variety of shapes and sizes. Some rather wealthier homesteaders were able to build substantial two-storey structures whereas the humblest of settlers contented themselves with dug-outs – shelters cut into a bank with a sod wall built up at the front.

Many women came to hate the problems created by sod houses but they remained in use long after imported timber became available for building timber-frame houses.

Most sod houses were single room structures but, by hanging a curtain across, some privacy could be created. Luxuries included caged birds (there were no songbirds on the Plains and the singing of a caged bird was a pleasant distraction) and potted plants. The sod house in the photograph below also boasts a pile of elk horns which was used for drying clothes.

Life on the Plains was one of constant hardship. To many, the hardest part was adapting to life in a sod house. Although in many ways ideally suited to the Plains – being cheap, easy to build and almost fireproof – the 'soddie' was also likely to be dirty, dusty, wet and cramped. Despite these problems many people continued to build and occupy sod houses long after timber became available to replace them.

Did you know?

Because homesteads on the Plains were so far removed from the shops in the east salesmen developed the first mail-order businesses selling goods from glossy catalogues called wish books.

▲ *A Nebraska soddie*

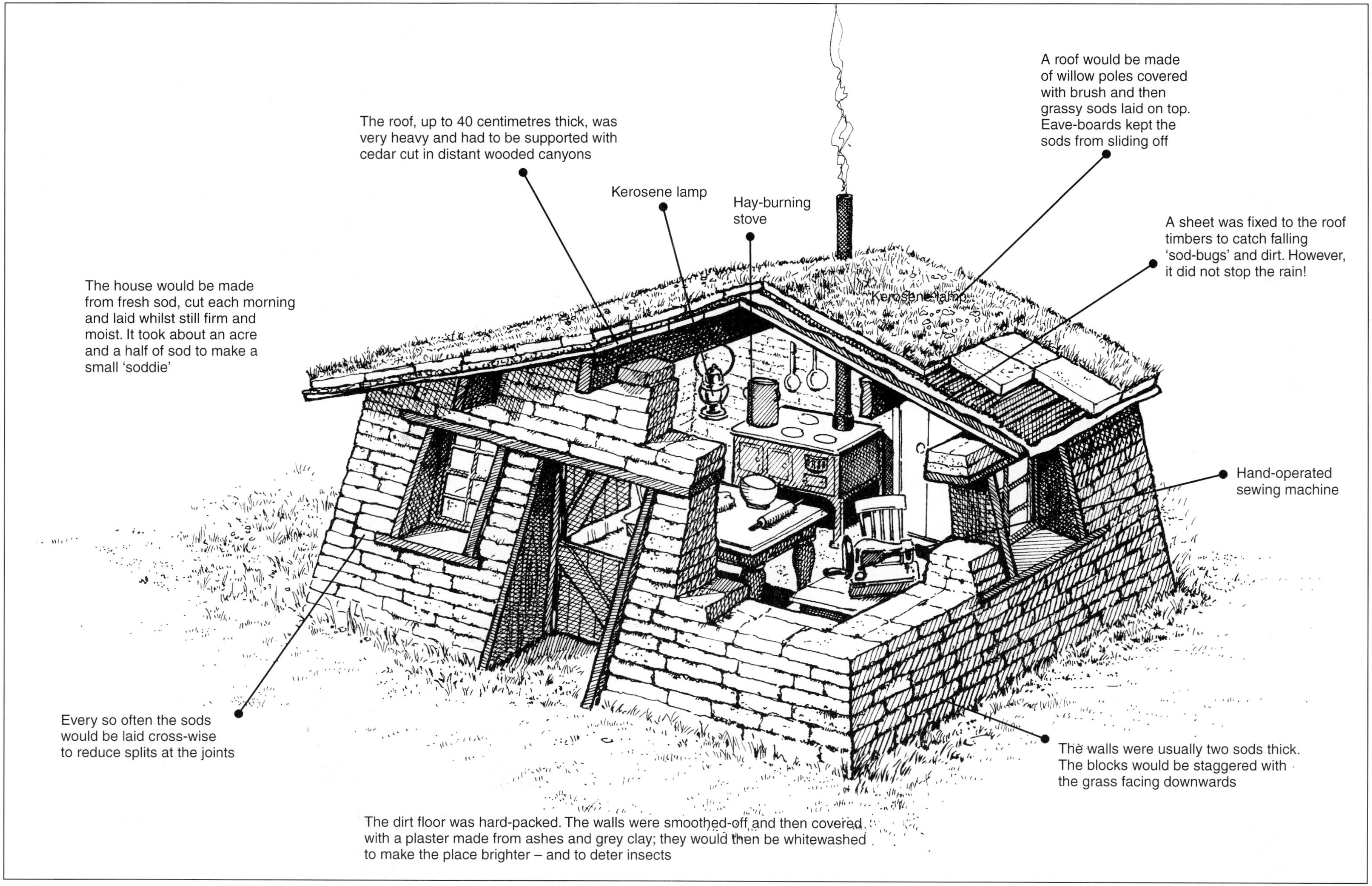

▲ *The structure of a sod house*

SOURCE A

My wife became unhappy for the first time when she saw bedbugs racing up the walls. She had a good, thick whitewash and up and plastered on the walls which got rid of the bugs.

Dr Cass Barns, a settler in Nebraska, 1878

SOURCE B

Oscar Babcock, a settler in Nebraska, built a sod dug-out which included a wooden door and a glass window. The whole structure cost less than $2.78 – a real bargain!

***The Story of the Great American West*, 1974**

SOURCE C

You did not have to keep dogs in order to have plenty of fleas. Just have a dirt floor and you have fleas for sure. They seem to spring from the dust of the earth.

Howard Ruede, a settler in Kansas, 1877

SOURCE D

Sometimes the water would drip on the stove while I was cooking and I would have to keep tight lids on the pans to stop mud from falling into the food.

A prairie wife recalls cooking in a sod-house

SOURCE E

The earth was an excellent insulator making a sod-house cool in summer and relatively easy to keep warm in winter.

***The Story of the Great American West*, 1974**

SOURCE F

The sod-house offered so many advantages that settlers continued to build them long after imported timber became available for building wooden frame houses.

H Horn, *The Pioneers*, 1974

SOURCE G

Contagious diseases were common. The shared drinking cup, the open well, the outdoor toilet (or no toilet at all) shared the blame with the lack of ventilation and crowded quarters of the sod-house.

Dr Cass Barns, a settler in Nebraska, 1878

SOURCE H

The soddie required very little maintenance and was almost indestructible. It even gave protection against the fierce prairie fires.

***The Story of the Great American West*, 1974**

▲ *A family wearing their Sunday best for a photograph, Kansas c.1865*

things **to do**

Task 1:

Read the sources on the previous page. These tell you some of the *advantages* and *disadvantages* of sod houses. Using the information from the sources complete the chart below.

Advantages	Disadvantages

Task 2:

Using the information in the sources, and your own knowledge, answer the following question:

The soddies were often unhygienic and dirty. Why then did so many people continue to build and occupy them?

What was life like for women on the Plains?

In the established towns and cities of the American West life for the women was hard but not necessarily worse than the life they had left back in the east.

However, few women were prepared for a life on the Plains. Few families arrived on the Plains with more than the bare essentials. As a result, in addition to braving the harsh climate of the Plains, women had to overcome acute shortages of even the most basic home comforts. Candles were essential for lighting the long, dark nights. These had to be handmade by continually dipping a wick into melted fat. Soap was made by mixing fat with water which had been passed through wood ash – the mixture was then boiled to produce soap. Clothes either had to be made (if the material was available) or, more typically, repaired. Fuel was essential to keep the fires lit but there were few trees on the Plains. Instead women had to gather up dried buffalo (or cow) dung to burn. These were known as buffalo chips.

▲ *A photograph showing a woman collecting 'buffalo' chips for fuel*

Once the fire had been lit food needed to be prepared. This could involve skinning and preparing meat as well as cooking it.

Many women were depressed by the lack of neighbours. Towns could be a very long way away and schools and public buildings were often unheard-of luxuries. Many women were driven to despair.

THE STORY OF SARAH SIM

Sarah Sim and her husband, Francis, left New England in 1856 to set up a new life on the Plains. They bought 160 acres of land in Nebraska. They were lucky – their land had a brook, a few trees and some neighbours nearby. Sarah was then 32 and had three children.

Sarah and her husband built a small cabin 10 feet by 10 feet and moved in with their three cows, two oxen, a horse, pigs and hens. The weather was dry, the water was hard and the wind blew continually.

Soon after, Sarah's second child died of whooping cough. Sarah's hand was injured and became infected – a finger was amputated. Her husband became ill and the weather worsened as winter approached. Sarah wrote in her diary, 'It almost breaks our spirits down. Pray for me that I may overcome my present fear'. But things did not improve and Sarah became deeply disturbed. For eight months she tore at her clothes, bit herself and the children, broke the windows and smashed up their belongings. She even attempted suicide. In desperation Francis tied her to the bed.

Slowly Sarah began to recover. She wrote in her diary, 'I sometimes quite despair, I would do anything to get better'.

The second winter in their new home was easier. Francis was fully fit again and had extended the cabin giving them more room. They planted new crops of potatoes and corn which did well. They even had enough salted pork to offer for sale.

Sarah still faced further tragedies. Four more of her children were to die of diphtheria and mumps but never again did Sarah become as depressed as she had been that first winter.

Did you know?

Good health in the American West was very difficult to maintain. Even small injuries could easily become infected and there were no antiseptics. Doctors were expensive and often far away. Even if a doctor was available, medicines still had to be found and paid for.

things **to do**

- **Task 1:**
Read the information in this investigation which tells you about the experiences of women on the Plains. Try to find as many of the problems that the women faced as you can and record them on the chart below. Then, in the next column, try to identify how they solved the problems.

Problems	Solutions
e.g. lack of clothing and material	*Needed to keep repairing things*

- **Task 2:**
The story of Sarah Sim is real and is based on her diaries. Use the information from this investigation, and your own knowledge, to answer the following question:
What was life like for women on the Plains?

What problems did the homesteaders face and how did they deal with them?

things **to do**

- **Task 1:**
  Cut out the cards on the following pages.

  Try to match the solutions to the problems faced. *Remember: not every problem can have a solution.*

  Which problems could not be solved?
  Many people found these remaining problems too much to cope with. Some homesteaders starved to death. Many were forced to sell their land in order to survive. Others became tenants on their own land. Between 1889 and 1893, 11,000 homesteads were repossessed in Kansas alone.

- **Task 2:**
  Using the information in this investigation, and your own knowledge, answer the following question:
  What problems did the homesteaders face and how successful were they in overcoming them?

PROBLEM CARDS

Gathering of crops required long and backbreaking effort. There were very few labourers available to help.	The ground on the Plains was very hard. Ordinary ploughs either broke or failed to scratch the surface.
'This,' said a newcomer to the Plains, 'would be a fine country if we just had water.' 'Yes,' said the other man heading east, 'so would Hell.' (A popular folk story.)	Summer saw droughts with the temperature over 100°F (approximately 37°C) for weeks on end. This could scorch a corn crop as effectively as a blowtorch.
In winter temperatures could plunge to as low as −40°F (−40°C) and both people and animals could freeze to death.	The winter blew endlessly across the Plains, in winter and in summer, night and day.
Prairie fires could spread quickly in the hot, dry summers. If quick, a controlled fire could be lit in advance of the real fire to try and slow it down.	Lack of land was a problem. The Homestead Act of 1862 gave settlers 160 acres but this was not enough to support a family in the hot, dry climate.
Plagues of grasshoppers could descend and strip the land and any crops in a very short time.	Cattle strayed onto the crops because there was no effective way of fencing the Plains. There were not enough materials.

SOLUTION CARDS

The spread of railroads across the Plains meant that huge quantities of materials (wood, seeds, new machinery etc.) could be brought to the Plains.

▲ *Machinery greatly eased the pressures of farming*

The Timber and Culture Act of 1873 allowed homesteaders to claim a further 160 acres of land free if they agreed to plant half an acre of trees. This extra land allowed some families to survive.

Steel-tipped ploughs (known as sod-busters were introduced by John Deere. These ploughs could even penetrate the hard prairie soil.

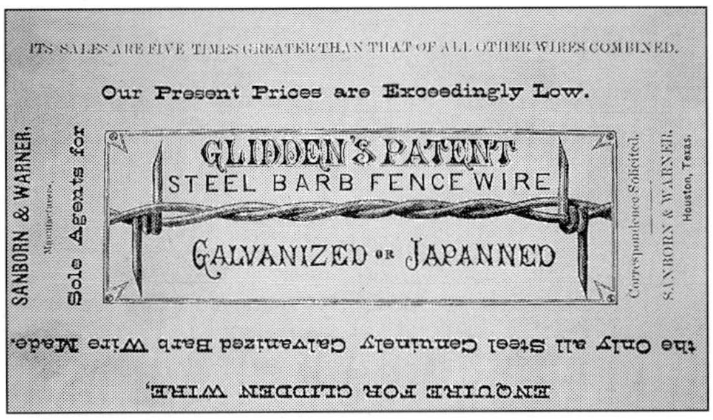

▲ *Barbed wire made fencing easy and cheap*

New crops were introduced which could withstand the lack of water. One of the most successful was Turkey Red Wheat which came from the Crimea (part of Russia) in 1874.

Dry-farming was introduced. Some fields would be left fallow to conserve moisture. Land would be ploughed after rain or snow and the surface would be covered with dust to stop the precious moisture from evaporating.

Wind pumps were invented which used the high winds of the Plains to draw up water from deep in the earth. Such pumps were very cheap to build.

The role of women on the Plains

issue **7**

the **big** picture

Key Question

How important were women on the Plains?

The popular movie image of women in the American West tends to limit their contribution to barroom hostesses or prostitutes. Only rarely does a woman feature in a leading role. Without doubt some women did do these jobs but the vast majority of women on the Plains formed the backbone of the new territories. In many ways these women led the way – for example they achieved the vote for women in Wyoming *50* years before women in Britain!

In addition to raising families and maintaining the home, women on the Plains established industries, ran newspapers, provided vital medical and educational services and campaigned for various causes. Some women became cowboys and still others turned to a life of crime as the photograph below shows. Pearl Hart won a name for herself as the west's last stagecoach robber (she also won herself a five-year sentence in an Arizona prison).

▲ *Cattle Annie and Little Britches, teenage members of the Doolin gang, both went to prison, then went straight*

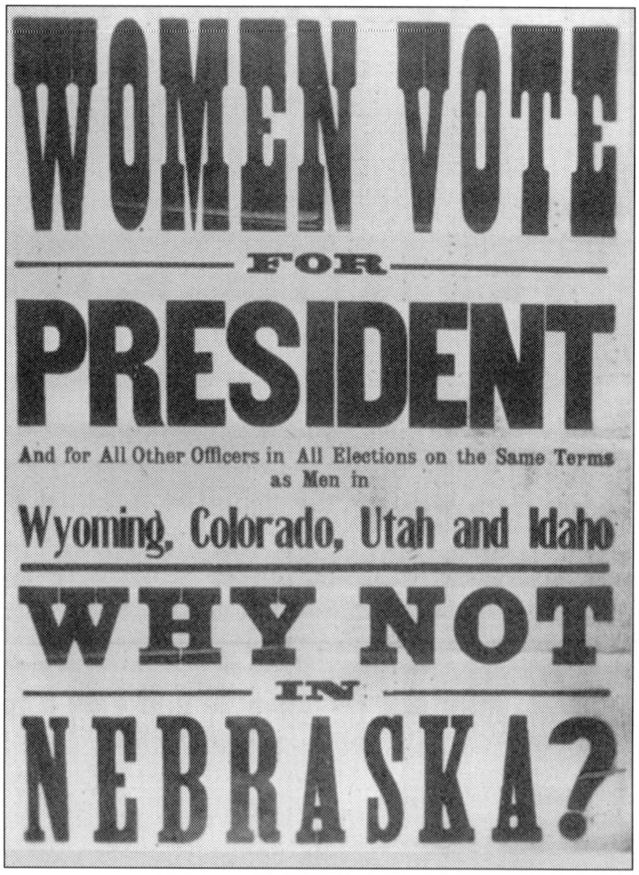

▲ *A poster from Nebraska used in the womens' campaign for the vote*

investigation 7.1 How important were women on the Plains?

In addition to raising families and supporting their husbands, many women made a name for themselves on the Plains:

- **Nellie Cashman** operated a chain of restaurants in many rough mining communities.
- **Abigail Scott Duniway** published a weekly newspaper for women. It was called *The New Northwest* and first appeared on 5 May 1871.
- **Caroline Churchill** founded a newspaper to promote equality for women. It was called *The Colorado Antelope* (but later renamed *The Queen Bee*) and first appeared in 1879.
- **Helen Clarke** helped manage the US Government's Indian programme. She assisted in the allocation of land on the Ponca reservation in the early 1890s.
- **Carry Nation** focused the attention of the whole nation on her activities. As part of her campaign against alcohol she had a habit of entering saloons with an axe and destroying them. Her work contributed to the period of Prohibition in America in the early twentieth century.
- **Martha Maxwell** was a crackshot who took to taxidermy (stuffing animals). She became so successful that she even displayed her work at the 1876 Centennial Exhibition in Philadelphia.
- Women formed the vast majority of teachers on the Plains. **Catharine Beecher** started recruiting women teachers as early as 1845 with her pamphlet *The Duty of American Women to their Country*:

  It is *woman* who is to come in and meet the demand for teachers. Woman, whom experience and testing have shown to be the best, as well as the cheapest, guardian and teacher of children.
- Mormon women in Utah established their own silk industry in 1877. Within a year they boasted five million silkworms. Mormon silk was successfully produced for the next 28 years and only ceased production because of cheaper, foreign imports.
- Many women on the Plains survived boredom, isolation, dirt, disease, lack of fuel and materials in order to keep their homesteads running.
- Women in Wyoming Territory gained the vote (and equality) in 1869 – some 50 years before their British counterparts!
- Many women served as missionaries bringing Christianity and education to the Indians.

things **to do**

- **Task 1:**
  Look carefully at the information on the previous page. Add the different jobs women did to the spider diagram below.

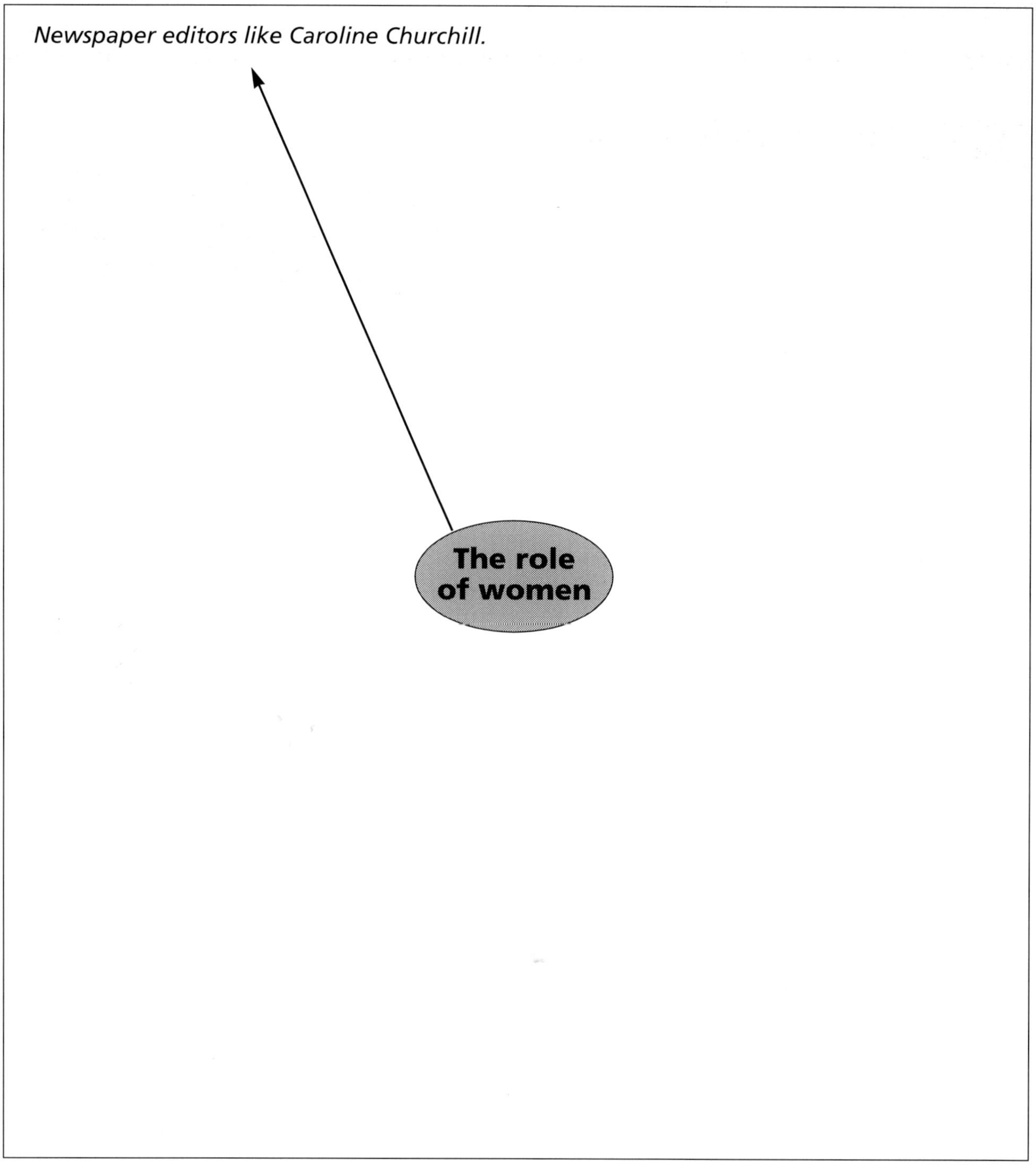

- **Task 2:**
  Using the information from this investigation, and your own knowledge, answer the following question:
  'Women played a vital role in settling the Great Plains.'
  Do you agree? Explain your answer.

issue 8

The impact of the railroads on the Plains

the **big** picture

Key Question

- What impact did the railroads have on the settlement of the Plains?

▲ *A steam engine of the Central Pacific Railroad*

The spread of the railroads across the Great Plains was an important factor in establishing White settlement but the railroads were equally important in bringing about the end of the traditional lifestyle of the Indians.

The railroads transported cattle, logs, farm produce and people onto and off the Plains and built extensive new towns to make the exercise profitable. As James Jerome Hill (an important railroad builder) said, 'the prairie without a population is a desert'. So successful were the railroads that, in Kansas alone, between 1870 and 1874, the population increased from 364,000 to 530,000. By 1880 western railroads were earning nearly three-quarters of their income from local traffic (i.e. from people already living there).

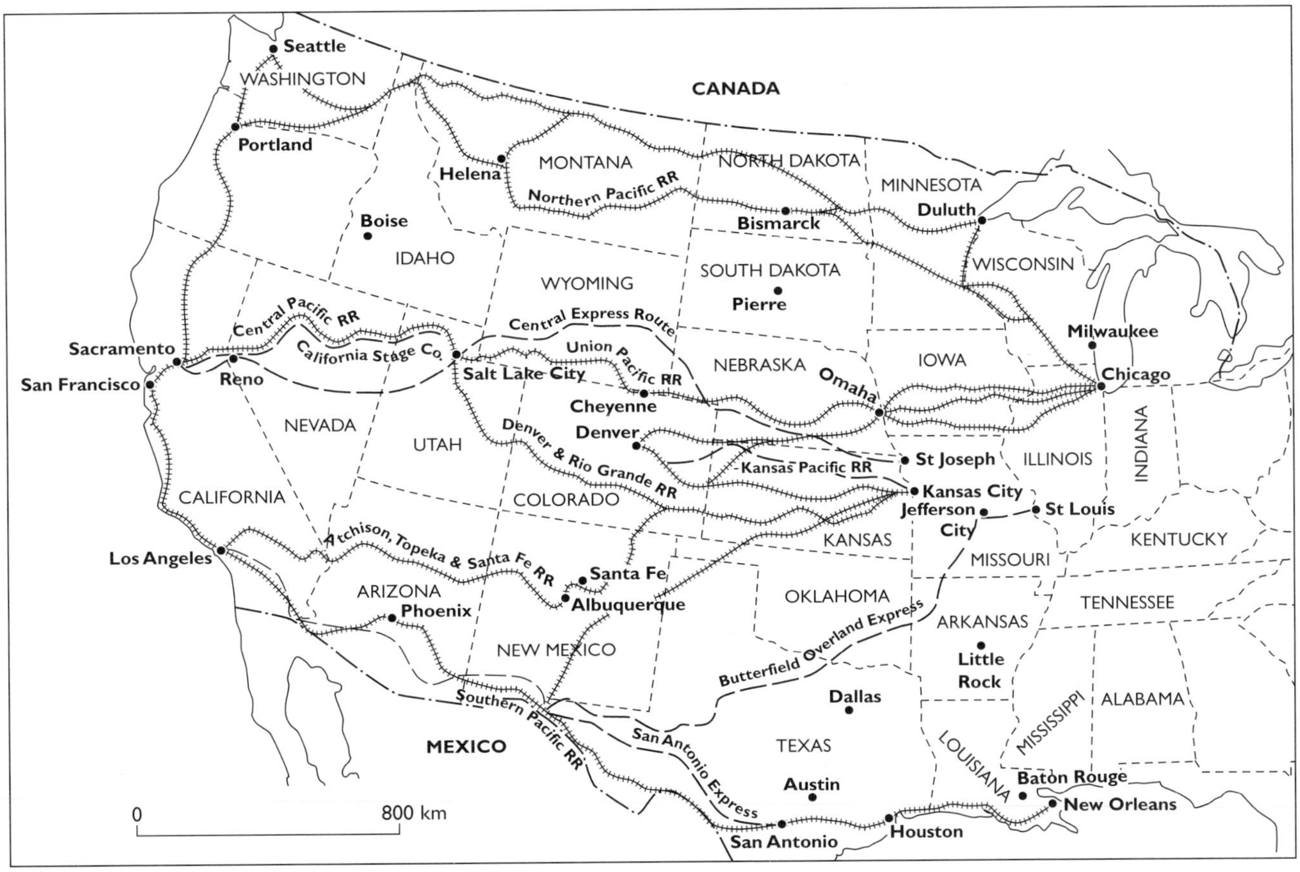

▲ *A map showing major railways and land routes after 1875*

investigation 8.1 What impact did the railroads have on the settlement of the Plains?

The railroads led to many changes – for the natives of the Plains as well as the White settlers. Many of the effects of the spread of the railroads are shown on this page.

Railroads allowed better and faster communication.

They allowed more effective law and order – it was easier to pursue criminals!

Railroads restricted the movement of Indians across the Plains.

The railroads brought settlers onto Indian land.

Railroads allowed quick and easy trade with the east.

Railroads provided jobs on the Plains.

The railroads split Indian lands.

Buffalo were killed to feed the railroad workers and by passengers on the trains for fun.

The railroads provided a link between both coasts of America.

Railroads made it easier for the army to chase the Indians.

Railroads encouraged the spread of cattle onto the Great Plains.

The railroads frightened off the buffalo.

The railroads brought raw materials (e.g. food, wood, seeds and machinery) to help settlers on the Plains.

Railroad companies encouraged the growth of towns with leaflets and special offers.

Railroads sold off unused land to make new towns.

things **to do**

- **Task 1:**
  Read the comments on the effects of the railroads which have been jumbled up on the previous page.

  Below are two boxes which form the basis of spider diagrams. Decide whether each statement on the previous page is a *positive* effect of the railroads or a *negative* one and add it to the appropriate diagram (an example has been added to help you).

1

Railroads provided jobs on the Plains.

Positive

2

Negative

things **to do**

- **Task 2:**
Look carefully at the two spider diagrams. Who appears to have gained from the railroads and who seems to have lost?

- **Task 3:**
Use the evidence you have collected from this investigation, and your own knowledge, to answer the following question:
The railroads brought only benefits to the Great Plains.
Do you agree? Explain your answer.

Did you know?

In 1861 there were only 30,000 miles (50,000 km) of railroads in the United States – all in the east. By 1900 there was over 200,000 miles (320,000 km) of railroads.

▲ *Although some trains were deliberately derailed, many more were wrecked by accident on the single-track western lines*

issue 9

Government, law and order on the Plains

the big picture

Key Questions

- How wild was the west?
- How important was the US Government in the settlement of the Plains?

The image of 'the Wild West' as seen in the movies is not a completely accurate one. There were gunfights (but more people were actually shot in the back) and there were some cold-blooded killers: Bill Longley killed 32 people by the age of 27 and John Wesley Hardin had killed 44 when he was finally jailed aged just 25. These men were the exception however – the bulk of the population was law-abiding.

Where new settlements arose in the new territories the people tended to adopt an unwritten set of rules that became known as the 'Code of the West'. A person fed a visitor because he, too, might be in need of food in the future; he asked no questions of a stranger because he, too, might have secrets to hide; he returned stray cattle because his cattle might also wander.

Many communities preferred to have the 'Code' a little more precisely defined. Mining settlements often agreed their own laws and set up Miners' Courts to enforce them. Where people chose to ignore the accepted laws vigilante groups of local citizens were set up to apprehend the offenders and ensure that they did not reoffend – this was usually achieved by hanging.

Some attempts to enforce law on the Plains became legendary. One such attempt was the work of Judge Roy Bean who advertised himself as 'the Law West of the Pecos'.

Judge Roy Bean began his career in law enforcement at the age of 56, shortly after opening a saloon in the Texas wilderness. Being 200 miles from the nearest court, and since Roy Bean was a fairly responsible citizen, Texas Rangers began bringing him their prisoners for judgement. His knowledge of the law was always erratic and some of his decisions even more so.

▲ *Judge Roy Bean presides at his court*

On one occasion an Irish railroad labourer stood accused of murdering a Chinese man. Several hundred of the Irishman's colleagues turned up to ensure fair play. Nervously the judge flicked through his law books and announced his verdict – there was a lot about killing men but there was nothing that specifically said it was wrong to kill a Chinese man so, case dismissed!

It often took quite a while to establish law and order in the new territories. When official law enforcement officers were appointed they often had a huge job to undertake – not necessarily in terms of the amount of crime they had to deal with, but in terms of the huge areas they had to cover and the low wages they were paid.

US Marshal
Responsible for law across a whole territory. Supported by federal judges, the Marshal enforced federal laws assisted by:

Deputy US Marshals

Deputy US Marshals

County Sheriff
Responsible for law within their county only. In addition to peace keeping the sheriff also had responsibility for the maintenance of the county jail and dog pound. The sheriff could call on a number of:

Deputy Sheriffs

Deputy Sheriffs

Town Marshals/Chiefs of Police
These people were appointed to keep the peace within a town and had no jurisdiction outside town.

▲ *The official hierarchy of law enforcement was headed by the US Marshal as the diagram above shows*

investigation 9.1 How wild was the west?

The following sources show examples of law and order in the west:

SOURCE A

▲ *The bodies of Grant, Bob and Bill Dalton with Dick Broadwell – members of the Dalton gang killed by members of the public as they tried to rob two banks in Coffeyville, Kansas, 1892*

SOURCE B

▲ *Marshal Henry Brown and associates under arrest after attempting a bank robbery, Caldwell, Kansas*

SOURCE C

The practice of drawing deadly weapons, except as a last resort for the defence of life, is forbidden, being dangerous to society. Notice is given that all offenders against this regulation will be dealt with.

Vigilance Committee,
Virginia City, Montana
23 September 1865

A warning to potentially violent people telling of the consequences of such behaviour

SOURCE D

The town of Abilene, Kansas, was opened as a 'cow town' by Joseph McCoy in 1867. The town depended on the cattle industry for its existence. By the end of January 1872 the people of Abilene had voted to ban cowboys from the town because of the noise and damage they caused.

From the records of the town

SOURCE E

▲ *Dave Mather, Assistant Marshal of Dodge City, Kansas*

SOURCE F

▲ *Three men charged with murder and hung by a vigilante group*

SOURCE G

▲ *Men of the Texas Rangers – originally set up by the Mexicans to keep the peace in Texas*

SOURCE H

Did you know?

Robert Charles Bolton was commonly known as 'Black Bart'. He was a stagecoach robber who bragged that he never harmed anyone. He had an educated voice and always left poetry in the stagecoaches that he robbed.

▲ *The main street of Dodge City in 1878. The sign nailed to the town well says 'The carrying of fire arms is strictly prohibited'*

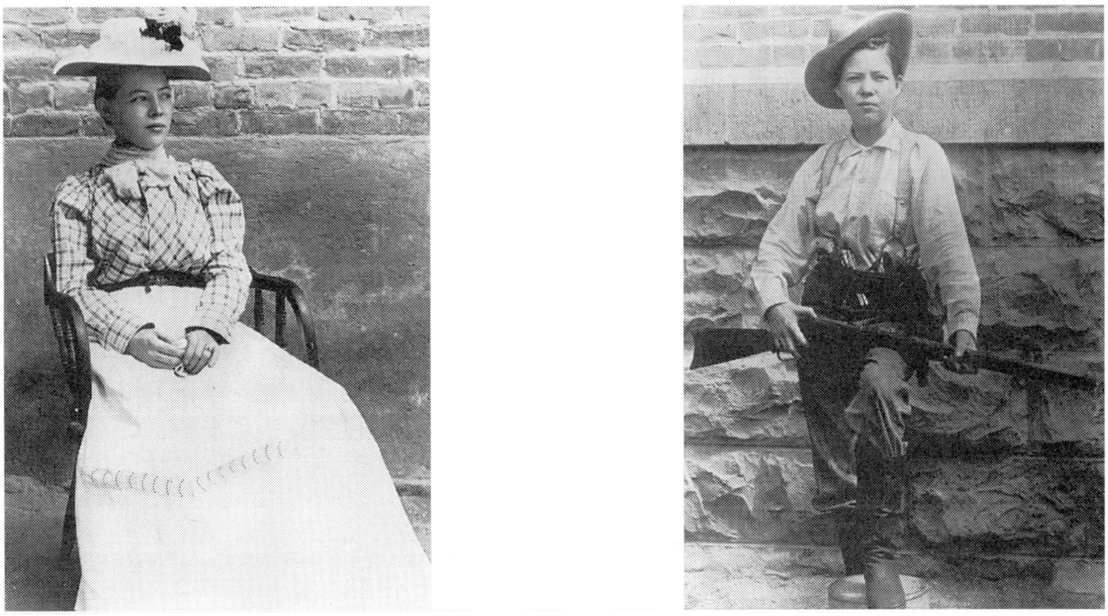

▲ *Appearances can be deceptive. Pearl Hart was serving a jail sentence when these 'before and after' photographs were taken. She was the last stagecoach bandit in the US*

things **to do**

The sources A–H on the previous pages all show examples of law and order in the west. They show law and order at every level – state and locally appointed lawmen, vigilante groups, semi-official organisations like the Texas Rangers and the results of actions carried out by ordinary, law-abiding people.

- **Task 1:**
  Complete the chart below by giving examples of the law enforcement offered at each level.

Organised by state	**Organised by town or county**
Unofficial measures	**Actions of ordinary people**

- **Task 2:**
  Using the evidence from this investigation, and your own knowledge, answer the following question:
  The west was a lawless place.
  Do you agree? Explain your answer.

investigation 9.2 How important was the US Government in the settlement of the Plains?

The US Government played a major role in the settlement of the Plains but there were other factors which encouraged settlement as well:

The role of the US Government

- The Government sent expeditions onto the Plains to assess their suitability for settlement.
- They provided laws to help the settlers such as the Homestead Act of 1862 and the Timber and Culture Act of 1873.
- The Government allocated lands for settlement in the new territories.
- They promoted the spread of railroads which brought goods and people from the east.
- The US Army was provided to protect the settlers.
- The Government moved the Indians onto reservations.
- The Government provided a political and legal structure for the new settlements.

There were also many other factors which encouraged settlers onto the Plains:

Other factors

Greed – the discovery of gold in California and, later on, in Colorado and the Black Hills brought thousands of miners onto the Plains.

Greed – books like Brisbin's *The Beef Bonanza – How to get rich on the Plains* encouraged people to move to the Plains.

Various groups (like the Mormons) were escaping from persecution in the east.

Population pressures in the east, along with overcrowding, encouraged people to move west.

The mystery of the west offered a new beginning for some people.

things **to do**

- **Task 1:**
  Using the information provided, and your own knowledge, answer the following question:
  Was the Government the most important factor in the settlement of the Great Plains?
  Explain your answer.

Did you know?

The fastest form of mail across the Plains (before the invention of the telegraph) was the Pony Express. Started in 1860 the Pony Express went from St Joseph, Missouri to Sacramento, California. There were 190 stations along the route and at each the riders were only allowed two minutes to change horses.

issue 10

The US Government and the Indian problem

the **big** picture

Key Questions

- Why were Indian and White lifestyles always leading to conflict?
- How did the US Government attempt to deal with the Indian problem?
- Sand Creek: victory or massacre?

The first White settlers to arrive in America found the Indians to be friendly and helpful but, as more and more Whites arrived, the Indians began to feel threatened.

The main threat to the Indians in the first decades of White settlement came not from acts of violence but from diseases, like measles and smallpox, to which the Indians had never been exposed. They had no natural immunity and thousands died – their medicine men were powerless against such diseases. Whole villages were wiped out or depopulated to such an extent that the survivors were unable to support themselves.

As still more Whites poured into America they began to encroach more and more on Indian land. The Indians could either fight, move further away to the west or adopt the White mans' customs and take up farming. The choice was not an easy one:

> Where today are the Pequot? Where are the Narragansett, the Mohican, the Pokanoket, and many other once powerful tribes of our people? They have vanished before the greed and oppression of the White man, as snow before a summer sun. Will we let ourselves be destroyed in turn without a struggle? Will we give up our homes, our country given to us by the Great Spirit, the graves of our dead, and everything that is dear to us?
>
> **Chief Tecumseh of the Shawnees**

In the early years of the nineteenth century the Great Plains remained an area of mystery. Early maps show the area as a large white space marked 'Great American Desert – unexplored'. It was to be the final refuge for the Indians. As the Whites finally began to enter and exploit the Plains themselves the very survival of the Indians was in question.

investigation 10.1 Why were Indian and White lifestyles always leading to conflict?

Indian lifestyle

- The Indians were nomadic and followed the buffalo.
- The Indians did not believe in land ownership.
- The Indians had a strong sense of community – everyone depended on everyone else.
- The Indians were very religious and believed that the earth was sacred, having been put there by the Great Spirit.
- The Indians mutilated their enemies to handicap them in the next life.
- The Indians conserved the land and its resources out of respect for the Great Spirit and to keep up the stocks of buffalo etc.
- The Indians had no standing armies. Their warriors were also the heads of families and providers of food for the women and children.

White lifestyle

- The Whites had professional soldiers who fought their battles for them.
- The Whites stayed in one place and fenced off the land.
- The Whites regarded mutilation of the dead as barbaric.
- The land was seen merely as a resource to be used.
- White society tended to put the needs of the individual before those of the community.
- The Whites did not conserve the resources of the earth (like gold, timber etc.) but exploited them.
- The Whites believed in the idea of manifest destiny. The idea was that it was their destiny to occupy the Plains.

things **to do**

- **Task 1:**
  Look carefully at the diagrams on the previous page. Use that information, and your own knowledge, to compare the Indian and White lifestyles. Use the chart below to help you record your findings.

  You may want to add other areas for comparison.

	Indian	**White**
warfare	*Indians used hit-and-run guerrilla tactics*	*Whites used their armies to fight pitched battles*
land ownership		
conservation		
animals		
bravery		
religion		
religion		

- **Task 2:**
  Using the information from task 1, and your own knowledge, answer the following question:
  Why were Indian and White lifestyles always leading to conflict?
- **Task 3:**
  Using the information from the last two investigations, and your own knowledge, answer the following question:
  The land was the biggest cause of conflict between the Indians and the Whites.
  Do you agree? Explain your answer.
  NOTE: to answer this question properly you will need to consider most of the major areas of conflict between the two peoples in order to reach your conclusion. The sentence beginnings below may help you to organise your thoughts.

> There were many areas of conflict between the Whites and Indians. These included . . .
>
> Some differences between the two peoples did not lead directly to war, for example . . .
>
> The Indians were very attached to the land because . . .
>
> The Whites felt differently about the land because . . .
>
> Overall I think that the land was/was not the biggest cause of conflict because . . .

investigation 10.2 How did the US Government attempt to deal with the Indian problem?

The attitude of the US Government to the Indians changed according to their views on the value of the Great Plains.

When the Plains were considered to be useless the Government was content to let the Indians have sole possession of the area. When gold was found in California, and new land acquired in Texas, the Plains became a vital link between the two halves of the expanding nation. The Indians were therefore moved onto land between the overland routes. When gold was discovered in the Black Hills (Dakota) and other areas, White people began to realise the true value of the Plains. The Indians became a nuisance to be either destroyed as vermin or confined to small pockets of land where they were dependent on the US Government for their survival. As the Indians fought back in desperation the Government declared war – not against the Indians but against their food supply, the buffalo.

The policies adopted by the US Government can be divided into:

- **Separation:** isolating the Indians in their own half of the country;
- **Concentration:** confining each Indian tribe to its own, defined area with the land in between used for White travellers to the west.
- **Reservation:** limiting the Indians to small parcels of land where they would remain, effectively, prisoners.
- **Destruction:** of the Indians' culture, lifestyle and food supply.

SEPARATION

The Permanent Frontier set up in 1832 was the first attempt by the Government to deal with the Indians. The idea was simply to separate Whites and Indians. As President Andrew Jackson explained:

> It is certain that the Indian tribes cannot exist surrounded by our settlements and in continual contact with our people. They have neither the intelligence, the industry, the moral habits, nor the desire to improve which are essential to any favourable change in their condition. If their disappearance is to be avoided it can only be done by a general removal beyond our boundary.

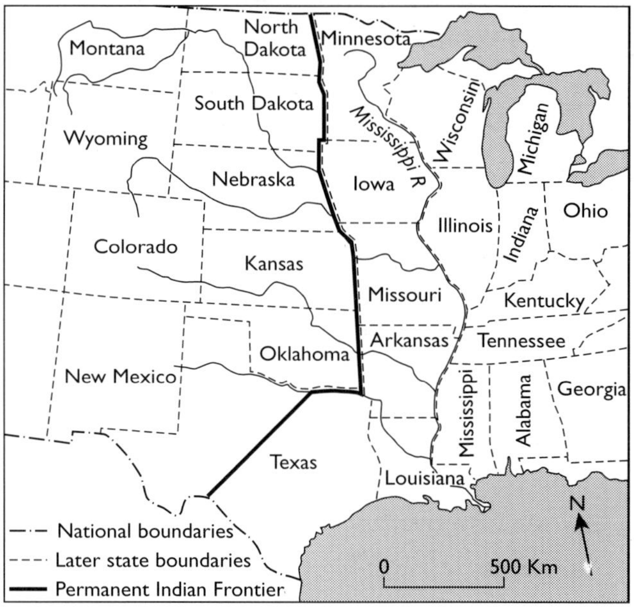

▲ *The Permanent Frontier*

The Government genuinely believed that this was the ideal and decent solution to the problem. To meet this goal all Indians living to the east of the Permanent Frontier were to be moved to the west. This caused horrendous hardship.

In 1836 Texas gained its independence from Mexico and thousands of Americans flocked to the new lands. In 1848 war against Mexico gave the United States even more land in the west and in 1849 gold was discovered in California. The Plains were now an obstacle to be crossed between the eastern and western coasts of the US. The Permanent Frontier lasted less than 20 years. The Indians were becoming more and more hostile – a new solution was needed.

CONCENTRATION

Thomas Fitzpatrick worked very closely with the Indians and had their trust. He clearly saw the threat of a full-scale war between the Whites and the Indians. In 1851, at Fort Laramie (Wyoming), he engineered a treaty between the Indians and the Whites. This treaty is known as the Treaty of Fort Laramie. It defined exactly the land allocated for each Indian tribe on the Plains, the routes for White travellers and the role of the US Army in keeping the peace.

Sadly, the peace did not last for long. There were many reasons why the peace ended:

- Increasing traffic across the Plains disturbed the buffalo and the Indians often left their allocated areas of land in order to hunt.
- Whites began to encroach on Indian land in the search for gold and to settle.
- In 1854 Indians killed a lame cow which had been left behind by a wagon train. When the owner found out he asked the army to see if the Indians could be made to pay for the cow. A young army officer named John Gratton handled the matter badly and the Indians were furious.
- In 1859 gold was discovered in Colorado and, by the end of the year, 25,000 miners had crossed Indian land to the new gold fields.
- The Indians were furious at the way the Whites continually broke the treaty and, in 1862, the Sioux, led by Chief Little Crow went on the warpath killing over 700 settlers. This is known as the Great Sioux Uprising.
- In 1864 a peaceful village of Cheyenne Indians at Sand Creek were attacked by the US Cavalry (see investigation 10.3).

Again, a new solution was needed. This time the Whites were becoming much less patient and there were those who argued that the Indians should be destroyed.

RESERVATION

In 1867 a meeting at Medicine Lodge Creek (Kansas) established a new policy. Some Whites, especially the army, wanted the Indians exterminated but this idea was rejected (partly on the grounds of cost – it was too expensive to pay the soldiers to hunt down and kill the Indians). Instead, the Indians would be confined to small pockets of land where, unable to hunt, they could be taught to farm. They would also get regular supplies of food from the Government.

Sadly this arrangement did not work either:

- The Government did not realise that the chiefs had no power to make the people follow them and many warriors continued to come and go as they wished.
- The Government appointed many agents to run the Indian reservations. Many of them were dishonest and gave the Indians only a fraction of what they were entitled to. Sometimes they sold the remainder to supplement their very low wages.
- Sometimes the agents swapped the meat for older, mouldy meat which they gave to the Indians:

> The greatest evil is that the Indians are poorly clothed and badly fed or starved. I doubt that there is a reservation in the country on which the average White labouring man would be content to live and survive on Indian rations. At the Crow-Creek Agency in 1863–4 the Indians reported several deaths from starvation; they were constantly begging for something to eat. Even worse was proven. It was shown that cows were used that had died natural deaths, and that meat was issued which stank and was full of maggots.
>
> **JP Dunn, *Massacres of the Mountains*, 1886**

- In 1868 Chief Red Cloud led his Indians against the Whites in what has become known as Red Cloud's War. He won a major victory and was granted the Great Sioux Reservation for his people. The US Government was eager for revenge.

DESTRUCTION

Alarmed and embarrassed by Red Cloud's victory the Government decided to destroy the Indians' power by destroying the Indian lifestyle and culture:

- In 1871 the Government began to destroy the influence of the chiefs by refusing to sign treaties with them.
- In the 1880s they set up tribal courts to bypass the power of the elders and the chiefs.
- In 1885 the Government abolished these Indian courts and US Federal courts took over control of the Indians.
- Indian tribes were mixed up on reservations to reduce tribal identity.
- Indian children were often removed from their parents and sent away to be educated in the culture of the White man. They were forced to learn English and could be beaten for speaking their own language.

▲ *Buffalo skulls were shipped to the Michigan Carbon Works to be crushed into fertiliser*

- The Government banned many important Indian ceremonies, for example the Sun Dance.
- The final Indian hope was the Ghost Dance religion and this was destroyed at Wounded Knee in 1890 when peaceful ghost dancers were massacred by the 7th Cavalry.

The Government also supported the efforts of hunters to destroy the Indians' principal food source – the buffalo. They allowed, and encouraged, hunters to go onto the Plains and kill as many buffalo as they could.

The numbers of buffalo crashed from an estimated 20 million in 1870 to around 1,000 by 1889. The Indians' means of survival on the Plains had gone forever.

things **to do**

- **Task 1:**
  Look carefully at the four different stages of US Government policy then complete the chart below.

Policy (what it tried to do)	Why it failed
1	1
2	2
3	3
4	

- **Task 2:**
  Draw a timeline in your books. Enter the dates of each policy and the main events which destroyed each policy.
  NOTE: policy 4 (destruction) did succeed hence the shaded section in the chart above.

- **Task 3:**
  Using the information from this investigation, and your own knowledge, answer the following question:
  Explain the failure of the US Government Indian policy between 1840 and 1890.

Sand Creek: victory or massacre?

We will not have the wagons which make a noise [trains] in the hunting ground of the buffalo. If the palefaces come further into our land, there will be scalps of your brethren in the tepees of the Cheyenne.

Roman Nose, Cheyenne Chief

In June of 1864 a settler named Ward Hungate, his wife, four-year-old daughter and baby were ambushed and killed by Cheyenne Indians near Denver, Colorado. The bodies had been scalped and mutilated.

Adapted from D. Nevin, *The Soldiers*, 1974

In February 1861 the US Government called the Cheyenne chiefs to a conference where they were forced to give up their lands and move to a small reservation near Sand Creek, Colorado. This was too much for many warriors to accept. As the railways advanced into Indian land, and hunters began to kill the buffalo to feed the railway workers, the Cheyenne retaliated.

The Cheyenne war lasted for three years before they began to look for peace. Black Kettle, an important peace chief, moved his people onto the Sand Creek reservation. The land around Sand Creek was poor and the Cheyenne were forced to leave the reservation or starve. They became so desperate that they started to attack wagon trains looking for food. As tension increased, Black Kettle and other peace chiefs moved their bands to Fort Lyon as a gesture of surrender. The commanding officer at Fort Lyon told them to camp along the bank of Sand Creek where they would be protected.

Meanwhile, Colonel John M Chivington (commander of the Military District of Colorado with the 1st and 3rd Regiments of Colorado Cavalry), decided to take revenge against the Cheyenne camp. At dawn on 29 November 1864 Chivington's men attacked the camp. What happened that day has been controversial ever since; some see it as an important victory over hostile Indians but others see it as a massacre of peaceful Indians.

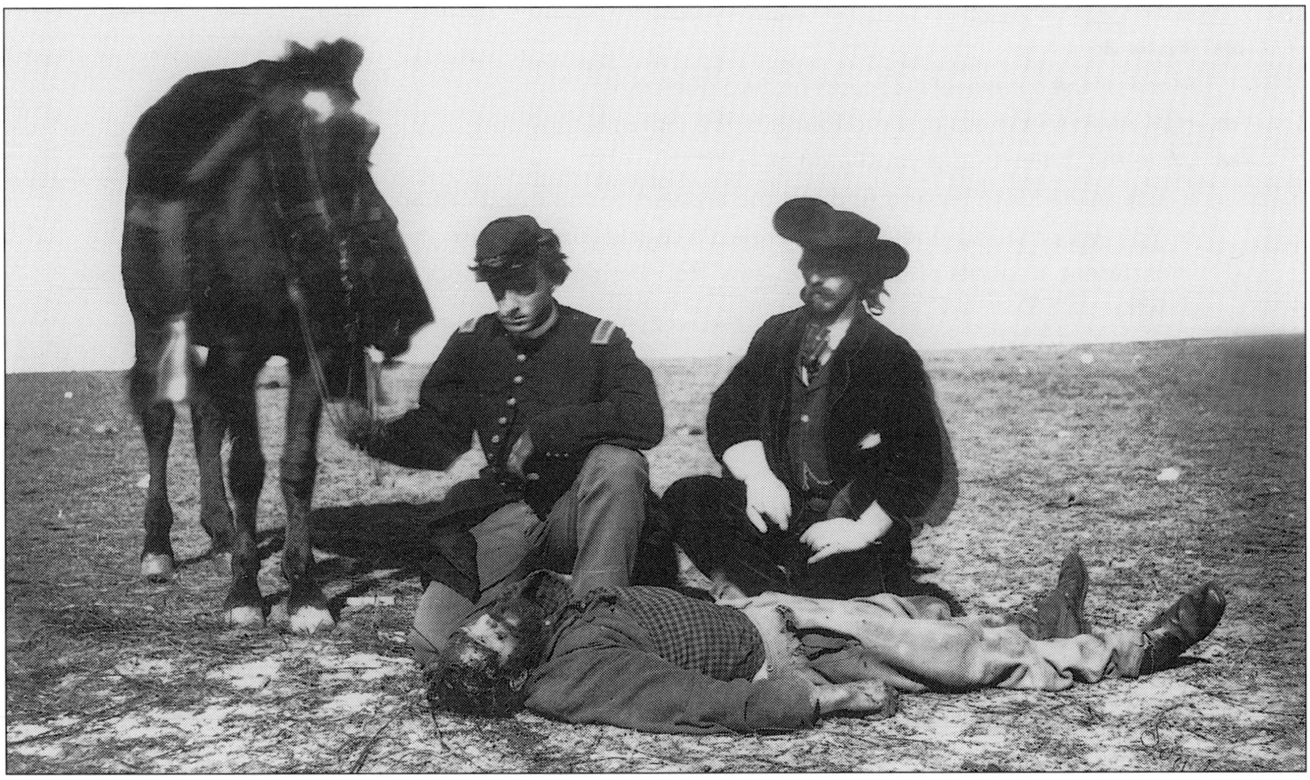

▲ *Soldiers examine the scalped body of a hunter killed by the Cheyenne*

KEY CHARACTERS

Colonel John Chivington: a former preacher and blacksmith who commanded the 3rd Colorado Cavalry – a regiment of men (largely Indian haters) who served for 100 days. News of the events at Sand Creek led to an enquiry which acquitted him, but he was relieved of command anyway.

Robert Bent: a man with Cheyenne blood (one of his parents was Cheyenne). He had been forced to guide Chivington's men.

John Smith: army interpreter. Worked as a trapper and married a Cheyenne woman. In time he became a respected member of the Cheyenne tribal council. Smith had gone to Black Kettle's camp, with Private Louderback of the 3rd Colorado to trade with the Indians. Smith's son, Jack, was killed by Chivington's men shortly after the battle at Sand Creek.

Black Kettle: an important peace chief of the Cheyenne. Despite Chivington's report of Black Kettle's death, he actually survived only to die on 27 November 1868 when his camp on the Washita was attacked by soldiers led by George Armstrong Custer.

things **to do**

You will need to cut out the cards on the following two pages before beginning these tasks.

IMPRESSIONS OF SAND CREEK

- **Task 1:**

  Some people see the events at Sand Creek as a justified attack on hostile Indians. Others see it as a massacre of peaceful Indians.

  Divide the cards on the following pages into those which suggest a *victory* and those which suggest a *massacre*.

- **Task 2:**

  Much of the controversy focuses on two questions:

- How many White scalps were found in the Indian camp? and
- Were the Indian bodies mutilated or not?

  a Use the cards to try and find out the answers to the questions above.

  b You will probably find it hard to reach a conclusion. Explain why there are so many different accounts of the same events. You should think about who said what, and possibly why.

IMPRESSIONS of SAND CREEK

GREAT BATTLE WITH INDIANS
THE SAVAGES DISPERSED
500 INDIANS KILLED
OUR LOSS 9 KILLED, 38 WOUNDED
***Rocky Mountain News*, 8 December 1864**

It was a mistake that there were any White scalps found in the village. I saw one, but it was very old, the hair being very faded.
Lieutenant J Cramer, 1st Colorado Cavalry

All acquitted themselves well. Colorado soldiers have again covered themselves with glory.
The Denver News

There was an unusual number of warriors present among the dead. Evidently they had assembled for some special purpose. I saw only one woman killed and no children.
Colonel JM Chivington

We found in the camp the scalps of 19 white persons.
Colonel JM Chivington at the Inquiry into the battle

I did not see any flags of peace or otherwise displayed by the Indians.
Captain P Talbot, 3rd Colorado Cavalry

At daylight this morning I attacked a Cheyenne village of 130 tepees, from 900 to 1,000 warriors strong. We killed Chiefs Black Kettle, White Antelope and Little Robe and between 400 and 500 others.
Colonel JM Chivington, official report

As we came within sight of the camp I saw an American flag. I also saw a white flag raised. Their flags were in so conspicuous a position they must have been seen.
Robert Bent, army guide

When troops began approaching I saw Black Kettle hoist the American flag fearing that there might be some doubt that the Indians were peaceful.
John Smith, interpreter

I saw a little boy still alive after the battle. A major took out his pistol and blew off the top of the boy's head. I counted 123 bodies. No more than 25 were men.
Corporal A Miksch, 1st Colorado Cavalry

Going over the battleground the next day I did not see a body of man, woman or child that was not scalped and in many instances their bodies were mutilated in the most horrible manner.
Lieutenant John Cannon, 1st NM Volunteers

Damn any man who sympathises with Indians. I have come here to kill Indians and believe it right and honourable to use any means under God's heaven to kill Indians.
Colonel JM Chivington before the battle

I have been informed by Captain Booth that he visited the battlefield and counted only 69 bodies. Others state that few, if any, more than that number were killed.
Major E Wynkoop, 1st Colorado Cavalry

What of the Indian blanket that was captured, fringed with White women's scalps? I stand by Sand Creek.
Colonel JM Chivington in a speech, 1883

IMPRESSIONS of SAND CREEK (CONTINUED)

We found a White man's scalp, not more than three days old in one of the tepees.
Colonel JM Chivington, official report immediately after the battle

I should estimate there were between 400 and 500 Indians killed. I counted 350. I think about half the dead were women and children. Nearly all were scalped.
A Bird, soldier, 1st Colorado Cavalry

A soldier came to the opening of the tepee and called my attention to some White scalps he held in his hand. My impression was that two or three of them were quite fresh.
Dr C Burdsal, Surgeon, 3rd Colorado Assistant Cavalry

I saw a good many white scalps there. Some looked old, others not so old and one that was quite fresh – not more than five to eight days old at the furthest.
Thaddeus Bell, soldier, 3rd Colorado Cavalry

All manner of mutilation was inflicted on the dead. They were scalped, their brains knocked out, women were ripped open, little children were clubbed to death with rifle butts.
John Smith, interpreter

I saw a camp of Indians with the Stars and Stripes [American flag] waving over the camp.
George Roan, soldier, 1st Colorado Cavalry

The entire Indian village was made up of not more than 500 people, two-thirds of which were women and children. The soldiers at Fort Lyon believed that the Indians were friendly.
D Louderback, soldier, 1st Colorado Cavalry

The scouting party returned reporting that they had counted 69 bodies. About two-thirds were women and children.
Major S Anthony, 1st Colorado Cavalry

I believe that between 500 and 600 Indians were killed. I counted 200 or more within a short distance of the camp. I counted about 12 or 15 women and a few children. I saw few bodies scalped.
Major J Downing, 1st Colorado Cavalry

I counted 450 dead Indian warriors. I saw only a small number of women killed. I saw one scalp of a White woman.
Sergeant S Decatur, 3rd Colorado Cavalry

The Plains wars: Custer and the Little Bighorn

the big picture

Key Questions

- Who was the real Custer?
- Why was Custer defeated?

Custer's defeat at the Little Bighorn has become a legend in the history of the American West. One reason for this is that every man in the five companies of the 7th Cavalry with Custer on that day was killed and so no one was able to tell the 'true' story of what happened. Most of the Indians did not even know that they were fighting Custer and few were willing to talk about what happened for fear of revenge.

THE BIGHORN CAMPAIGN

The discovery of gold in the sacred Black Hills of Dakota – the heart of Sioux land – brought huge numbers of miners onto Indian land. Unable to buy the land from the Sioux, the US Government set out to crush the Indians once and for all. The Bighorn Campaign was intended to end all Sioux resistance.

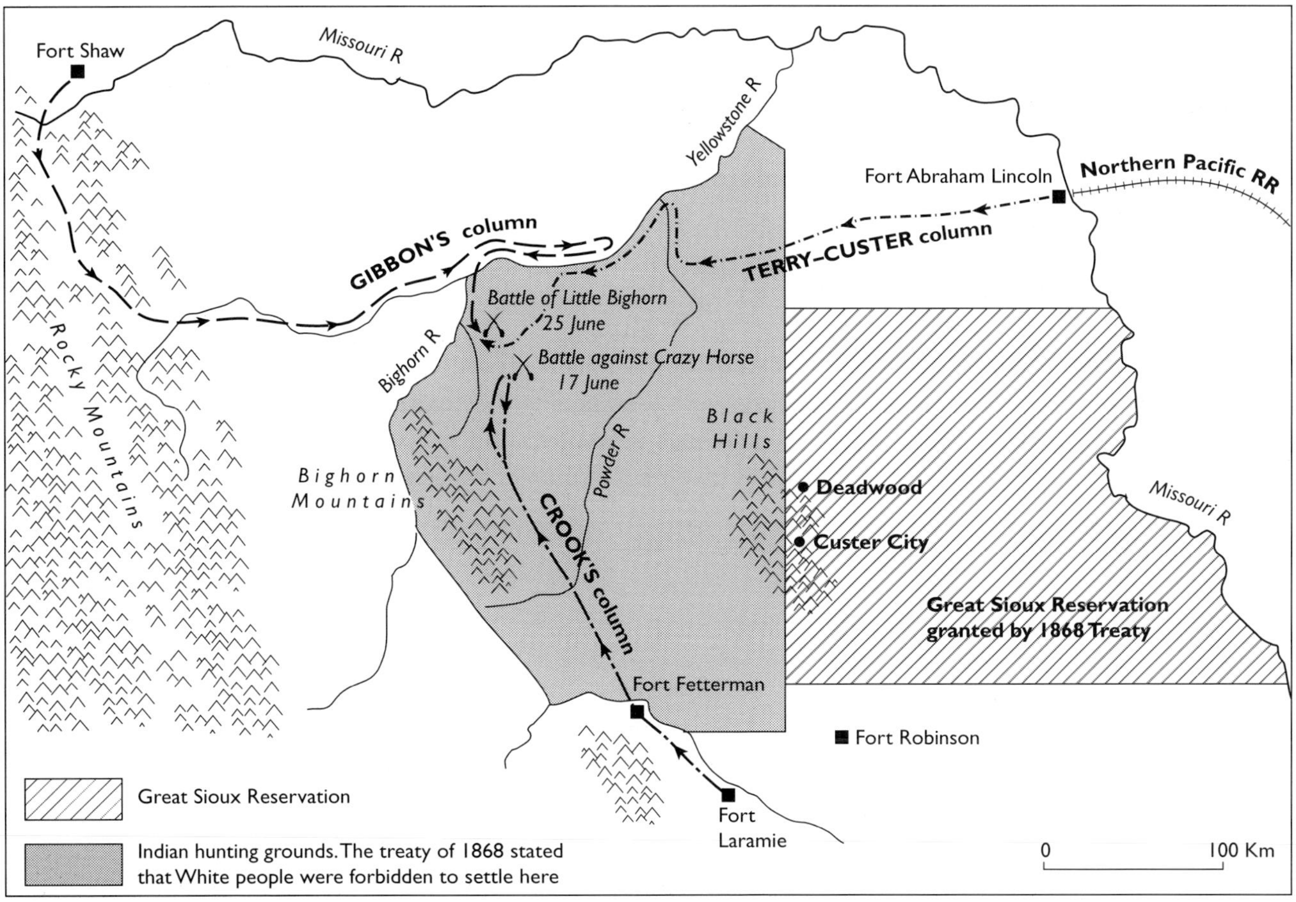

▲ *The strategy of the Bighorn Campaign*

THE ARCHAEOLOGICAL EVIDENCE

In 1983 a fire swept across the battlefield allowing archaeologists to do a very detailed study of the site. They dug up some of the grave markers and studied the bones underneath. They also recovered all metal objects (especially bullets and bullet cases) from the site. Each bullet has marks left on it by the gun that fired it (a bit like finger prints). Using these marks the archaeologists were able to estimate how many guns were used in the battle.

The archaeologists used the information from their study of the site to answer some of the questions posed by the lack of survivors.

Question	Answer
How many men did Custer have with him at the battle?	No one knows for certain. There were probably only around 210. The bodies of 28 men from 'E' Company were never found but there are already 252 graves.
Why are there so many graves?	It appears that the bodies were only lightly covered with branches and dirt at first. Animals soon dug up the bodies which then broke up. Bits of bodies rolled downhill and later gravestones were set up wherever bones were found – so some bodies got two gravestones.
What happened to 'E' Company?	Recent research shows that these men were trapped in a deep ravine where they were killed. The sides of the ravine then collapsed on top of the bodies, hiding them.
How many Indians were there?	A study of the bullets recovered shows that at least 750 Indian guns were used against Custer's men. Many other Indians would have used bows and arrows. Others would have used guns taken from soldiers already killed.

Did you know?

Although most pictures of the Battle of the Little Bighorn show the soldiers with sabres, they did not in fact have any – they had been collected in before the battle began.

A study of where things were found on the battlefield can also tell us exactly what happened to Custer and his men:

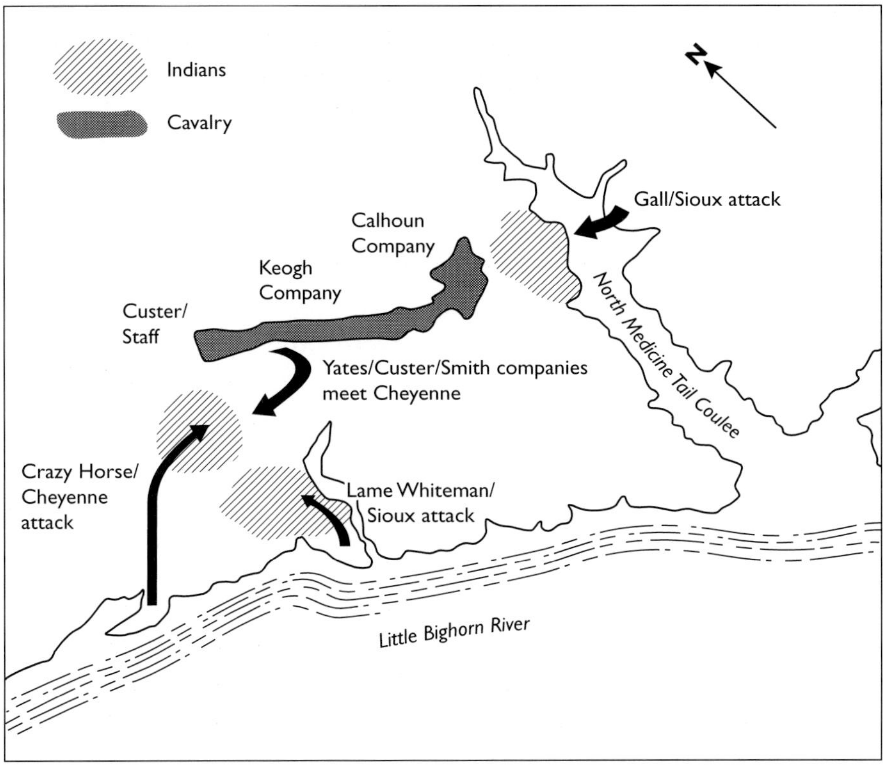

◀ *A map showing the early stages of the battle*

The Indians see Custer's men and pour across the river to attack. Custer's men form a line of battle along a ridge now known as Custer's Ridge.

What the evidence cannot tell us is *why* Custer was defeated.

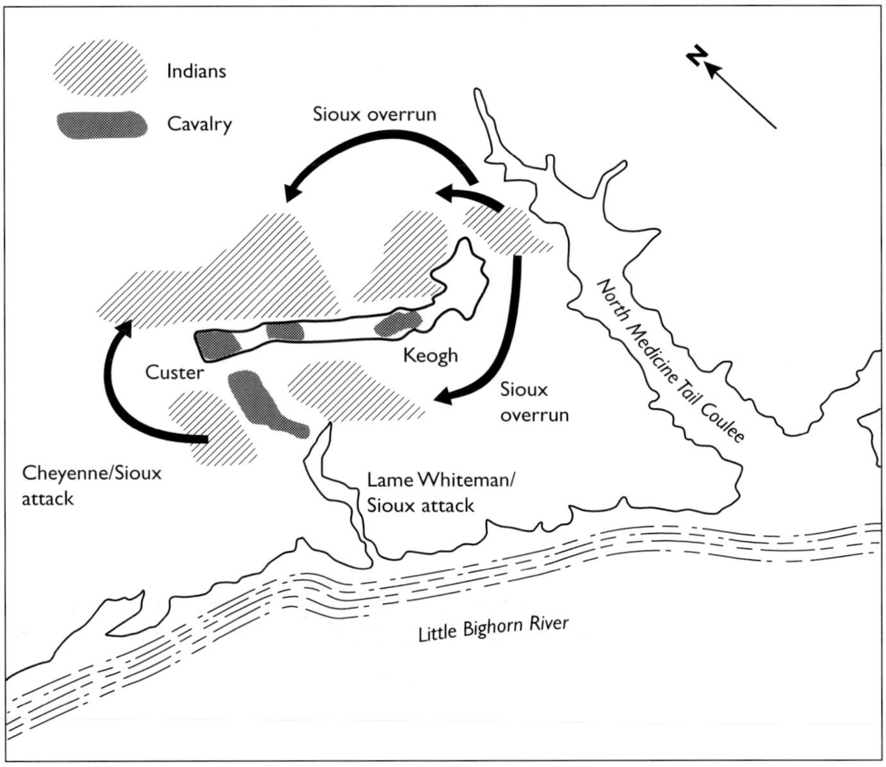

◀ *A map showing the final stages of the battle*

As more Indians arrive they begin to surround the soldiers who are forced to fight in smaller and smaller groups until all are killed.

TIMELINE OF EVENTS

Date			What happened
1868:	November 4		The Great Sioux Reservation (including the Black Hills) is created as part of the treaty which ended Red Cloud's War. It would be Indian land for ever!
1874:			Custer leads an expedition into the Black Hills. Gold is discovered.
1875:	Spring		A new gold rush begins. At first soldiers try to stop the miners but there are too many. When this fails they protect the miners against Indian attacks instead.
	Summer		The US Government tries to buy the Black Hills from the Sioux. Red Cloud suggests a price of $600,000,000! This angers the US Government who decide to act.
	December		Messages are sent to the Sioux ordering them to return to their reservations by 31 January 1876 or be declared 'hostile' (i.e. enemies).
1876:	February		The bands of Sitting Bull and Crazy Horse, along with many other Indians, do not report back. Instead, they gather in the Bighorn Mountains. Plans are made by the US Government to attack them.
	June		Three army columns are sent from three different directions to trap and destroy the Indians. The columns are led by Generals Crook, Gibbons and Terry.
	June 17		General Crook's column is attacked by Crazy Horse and forced to turn back.
	June 22		General Terry orders Custer and the 7th Cavalry to move ahead of the column to locate the Indian camp and prevent the Indians from escaping.
	June 24		Custer's scouts locate the Indian village.
	June 25		Custer decides to attack the Indian village. He divides the 7th Cavalry into three groups. Custer will lead the largest group. Officers Reno and Benteen will lead the others.
		3.00 pm	Reno's men charge towards the Indian village but they are forced back onto a tree-covered hill.
		3.45 pm	Custer begins to attack another part of the village. Large numbers of warriors move to surround him.
		4.15 pm	Benteen returns from searching for other Indians and joins Reno in the hills. Large numbers of Indians stop them from joining Custer several kilometres away.
		5.15 pm	Custer and his 210 men are probably all dead by now.
	June 27		Reno and Benteen are rescued as the Indians are driven away by the approach of General Gibbons' column.

investigation 11.1 Who was the real Custer?

SOURCE A

▲ *A photo of Custer wearing the uniform he designed himself*

SOURCE B

I am not impetuous or impulsive. Everything that I have ever done has been the result of the study that I have made of imaginary military situations that might arise. When I become engaged in campaign or battle everything that I have ever read or studied becomes focused in my mind as if the situation were under a magnifying glass and my decision was the instant result.

George Armstrong Custer

SOURCE C

Some officers were friendly and easy-going with their troops, but Custer struck me as being aloof and removed.

Sergeant Charles Windolf, 7th Cavalry

SOURCE D

A cold-blooded, untruthful and unprincipled man, despised by most of his officers.

General David Stanly, US Army

SOURCE E

The honour of his country weighed lightly in the scale against the 'glorious' name of George A Custer. The hardships and dangers to his men, as well as the probable loss of life were worthy of but little consideration when dim visions of promotion floated before the excited mind of our Lieutenant-Colonel.

Private Theodore Ewert, 7th Cavalry

SOURCE F

He was too hard on his men and horses. He changed his mind too often. He was always right. He never conferred enough with his officers. When he got an idea, we had to go!

Jacob Horner, 7th Cavalry

SOURCE G

I want to link my name not only to the present but to future generations.

George Armstrong Custer

SOURCE H

He was a brave warrior and died a brave man.

Low Dog (a chief at the Little Bighorn)

SOURCE I

▲ *Custer with the first grizzly bear he killed, 1874*

SOURCE J

Custer had a flair that caught the eyes of powerful men. Custer made perhaps the most extraordinary series of leaps in rank in the history of the US Army.

Between July 1862 and July 1863 he went from 1st Lieutenant (the lowest rank of officer) to Brigadier-General (one of the very highest ranks).

D Nevin, *The Soldiers*, 1974

SOURCE K

I know of no person more instrumental in bringing about the surrender of the Confederate Army at the end of the American Civil War than your most gallant husband.

General P Sheridan in a note to Custer's wife, Elizabeth

things **to do**

Task 1:

Look carefully at Sources A to K. Some of them give a positive view of Custer while others have a more negative view. Complete the chart below by adding *positive* statements or images in one column and *negative* in the other. An example has been added to help you.

Positive	Negative
Low Dog said Custer was very brave	

Task 2:

Custer saw himself as a hero but everyone else despised him.

Do you agree? Explain your answer with reference to the sources.

Task 3:

Using the sources in this investigation, and your own knowledge, answer the following question:

What sort of a person was George Armstrong Custer?

Did you know?

Custer was known by some Indians as 'Long Hair' but on campaign he always wore his hair short to stop it from becoming dirty.

investigation 11.2 Why was Custer defeated?

By the time you have completed this investigation you should be able to explain the roles of Custer, Reno, Benteen, Sitting Bull and Crazy Horse in Custer's defeat.

You should also be able to explain some of the causes of Custer's defeat and show how these causes link together.

things **to do**

At the end of this investigation you will find a series of cards. These give reasons why Custer was defeated. Some are due to things that happened on the day of the battle (**short-term causes**); others are due to things that happened before the battle (**long-term causes**); some are because of things that Custer did (**personal**); others are because of things over which Custer had no control (**impersonal**).

- **Task 1:**
  Using the cards, try to decide which of the causes are *short-term* and which are *long-term*. Make a note of your conclusions in the chart below.

Short-term	Long-term

- **Task 2:**
  Now try to decide which of the causes are *personal* and which are *impersonal*. Make a note of your conclusions in the chart below.

Personal	Impersonal

Did you know?

One horse, named Comanche and owned by Captain M Keogh, was found badly wounded after the Battle of the Little Bighorn. It was nursed back to health and became the mascot of the 7th Cavalry until its death (of old age) in 1892.

things **to do**

- **Task 3:**
  Using the information gathered in tasks 1 and 2 try to complete the columns in the chart below. It may help you to discuss your ideas with others in your class.

Soldiers' strengths	Custer's strengths	Indian strengths
Soldiers' weaknesses	**Custer's weaknesses**	**Indian weaknesses**

- **Task 4:**
  Using all of the information from the investigation, and your own knowledge, answer the following question in your exercise books:
  Why was Custer defeated at the Battle of the Little Bighorn?

REASONS FOR CUSTER'S DEFEAT

George Armstrong Custer finished his training at West Point. He was bottom of his class. He had a reputation for breaking rules and generally being sloppy.	In 1861 the American Civil War began. Custer was brave and soon rose to the high rank of Brigadier-General of cavalry.
Throughout the Civil War, and in later fights with Indians, Custer was never injured. This led him to believe in 'Custer's Luck'. He thought he was indestructible.	The Indians had become fed up of being chased and had decided to make a stand. This time they would not run but would stand and fight.
Some of Custer's men accused him of being too ambitious and keen to get promoted. This made him reckless. Others were annoyed that he kept plans to himself so no one really knew what they were doing.	In 1874 Custer found gold in the Black Hills – a sacred part of the Great Sioux reservation. Miners poured in. The Sioux blamed Custer and hated him.
The US Government could not stop the miners from entering the Black Hills so they tried instead to buy the land. The Indians refused to sell and both sides prepared for war.	The US Government ordered all Indians to return to their reservations by 31 January 1876 or prepare for war. The Indians chose to fight.
In 1875 Custer accused President Grant's brother of taking bribes. Grant was angry and took away Custer's command of the 7th Cavalry. Custer needed to get back in favour with the President.	Custer apologised to President Grant and got command of the 7th Cavalry back. He told friends he would try to 'cut loose' in order to restore his reputation.
The Indians at the Little Bighorn were led by very capable and brave leaders including Sitting Bull and Crazy Horse. The Indians were ready and able to fight.	The Indian camp at the Little Bighorn was one of the largest ever with over 12,000 Indians. Every soldier would be needed to defeat the Indians.
Custer was sent ahead to find the Indian camp. He refused extra men and guns because he wanted the 7th Cavalry to have all the glory for themselves.	Custer found the Indians on 24 June 1876. Next morning he set out to attack them before they could break camp and flee.
When Custer saw the Indian camp he shouted 'Hurrah! Custer's Luck'. He thought the Indians would be surprised and easy to defeat. He expected them to run away – they usually did!	Major Reno would attack one end of the camp; Custer would attack another part of the camp. Colonel Benteen was sent to look for other Indians to fight. This plan meant that the 7th Cavalry would be seriously weakened.

REASONS FOR CUSTER'S DEFEAT (CONTINUED)

Reno's men were forced back into the hills and surrounded. Benteen later joined Reno. Custer meanwhile appeared to attack the middle of the Indian camp by mistake and was soon attacked and surrounded.	Reno and Benteen were unable to leave their hill and so were unable to go to Custer's help. Custer was heavily outnumbered and was killed along with all of his men.
The Indians had modern rifles which could fire a number of bullets without reloading. The soldiers had single shot rifles and cartridges which split and jammed the rifles.	It was rare for so many different Indian peoples to come together. As a result their camp was vast and could not easily be attacked.
Custer decided to divide his men up rather than keep them together. Many people think that this was a mistake.	Custer was told 'Now Custer, don't be greedy. Wait for us'. Custer replied 'No, I won't'.
Personal	**Impersonal**
Short-term	**Long-term**

The defeat of the Plains Indians

issue 12

the big picture

Key Question

How were the Indians defeated?

The Battle of the Little Bighorn is often referred to as 'a victory in defeat' for the Indians. Although it clearly was a major victory it did not earn them the sympathy of the Whites. News of Custer's defeat reached Washington during the celebrations marking the centenary (100 years) of American independence.

The Whites called Custer's defeat a massacre and eagerly looked for revenge.

THE BEGINNING OF THE END

The first victims were the Indians already on the reservations. These people had taken no part in the battle. On 22 July 1876 the army took control of all Sioux reservations. They demanded that the Indians give up the Black Hills because they had broken the Treaty of 1868 by going to war against the Whites. To force the Indians to agree, the Government withdrew all rations for the Indians until they signed the Black Hills away – so they had no choice! The Sioux became prisoners at Fort Robinson.

Meanwhile army columns snaked across the Plains attacking Indians wherever they were found. Tired of running, Sitting Bull took his band to Canada. The soldiers however had located Dull Knife and his band and attacked at dawn. The survivors fled to join Crazy Horse. Crazy Horse had been promised a reservation along the Powder River and so eventually he surrendered. When nothing happened, Crazy Horse threatened to take his band away. He was immediately arrested and, during a scuffle, bayonetted in the stomach. He died on 5 September 1877 aged 35.

The Northern Cheyenne who lived near the Black Hills were rounded up and forced to move to Indian Territory (modern Oklahoma). There they were kept on poor rations and many died of malaria. Over the first winter they were forced to eat their own dogs to survive. On 9 September 1878, 237 men, women and children left the reservation led by Dull Knife and Little Wolf. Incensed, the army chased them through the harsh winter snows until they were eventually found. Many were killed.

In 1881 Sitting Bull returned from Canada and surrendered. He was held as a prisoner for two years before being moved to the Great Sioux reservation. There he became the principal chief of the Sioux but was unable to stop Government agents from persuading the Sioux to allow the break up of their reservation.

THE GHOST DANCE RELIGION

In 1890 news spread of a Paiute Indian who claimed to be God. He was named Wovoka. Wovoka talked to the Plains Indians about their dead relatives. He also taught the Indians a new dance. He said that God had returned to the Earth as an Indian to repair the damage done by the Whites. In the next spring new soil would cover the Earth burying the White men. Great herds of horses and buffalo would return, as would the ghosts of all dead relatives. The Ghost Dance, as it came to be known, soon spread across the Plains. The Indians were told that if they wore Ghost Shirts decorated with special patterns then nothing could hurt them. However, they were also told that they must not start to fight.

> You must not hurt anybody or do harm to anyone. You must not fight. Do always right.
> **Wovoka**

By mid-November Ghost Dancing had begun at every Sioux agency. No children went to school; no work was done; no crops were tended. The

Government officials panicked – not understanding the Ghost Dance's message of peace. Instead, the Government ordered the arrest of all Ghost Dance leaders. On 15 December 1890 Sitting Bull was arrested and a scuffle broke out during which he was shot dead.

THE MASSACRE AT WOUNDED KNEE

Many of Sitting Bull's followers fled to a camp under Chief Big Foot. Although desperately ill Big Foot ordered his followers to head for the reservation at Pine Ridge where he though they would be safe, protected by soldiers. After several days they were met by soldiers who escorted them to a camp near Wounded Knee Creek. The Indians settled down for the night surrounded by soldiers with powerful guns which could fire explosive shells. In the morning the soldiers attempted to disarm the Indians. No one is sure who fired the first shot but the soldiers opened fire. The powerful Hotchkiss guns fired explosive shells into the camp and in minutes Big Foot and more than half of his followers lay dead. The Indians were finally defeated.

The soldiers responsible for the massacre at Wounded Knee were members of Custer's old regiment – the 7th Cavalry. Custer had finally been avenged!

Did you know?

The last treaty signed between the Indians and the US Government was not signed until 1934. The Seminole Indians fled to Florida where they remained at war with the Americans until 1934.

investigation 12.1 How were the Indians defeated?

Read the information provided in the 'big picture' carefully.

things **to do**

- **Task 1:**
  Using the information provided in the 'big picture' complete the following chart showing what happened to the major individuals, and groups of Indians, after the Battle of the Little Bighorn.

What happened to . . .	
The Black Hills	
Chief Dull Knife	
Chief Crazy Horse	
Chief Sitting Bull	
The Great Sioux reservation	
The Northern Cheyenne	

- **Task 2:**
  In your exercise books produce a timeline from 1876 to 1890 showing the major events which led to the final defeat of the Indians at Wounded Knee.
- **Task 3:**
  Using the information in this investigation, and your own knowledge, answer the following question:
  The Ghost Dance religion preached peace. Why then did the US Government react so violently to it?

How successful was the US Government in the destruction of the Indians?

issue 13

the **big** picture

Key Questions

- Why did the US Government try to destroy the Indians?
- How do Indians live today?

Between 1870 and 1900 the US Government attempted to destroy the culture and lifestyle of the Indians by a series of measures. They attempted to:

- destroy the power of the chiefs by refusing to sign treaties with them;
- destroy the power of the Elders by setting up tribal courts to decide matters normally considered by the Elders;
- abolish the tribal courts (from 1885) and take direct control of Indian affairs;
- destroy the old, established tribal identities;
- remove children from their parents in order to educate them in distant boarding schools;
- abolish many traditional Indian ceremonies;
- reduce Indian land to a bare minimum in order to force the Indians to adopt a White lifestyle dependent on Government handouts;
- encourage hunters to destroy the vast buffalo herds which supplied the Indians with what they needed for survival;
- encourage White settlement all around the Indian lands to reduce the opportunities for Indians to leave the reservations;
- remove leading Indian chiefs either to distant prisons, or by killing them.

investigation 13.1 Why did the US Government try to destroy the Indians?

It would be wrong to think that the American people were either cruel or heartless. They felt that they were justified in the actions that they took against the Indians, and events such as the Battle of the Little Bighorn were evidence of this.

This investigation attempts to consider some of the reasons behind their actions. You may wish to look at issue 3 (The reasons for White Settlement on the Plains) for further ideas.

things **to do**

- **Task 1:**
  Using the information in this pack, and your own knowledge, attempt to complete the chart below by finding reasons for the actions shown. One has been filled in to help you.

Action	Reason
Destroying the power of the chiefs	*This would give more power to individual Indians and would be fairer*
Taking direct control over Indian affairs	
Destroying traditional tribal identities	
Removing children from their parents and sending them to boarding schools	
Banning ceremonies	
Removing or killing the leading Indian chiefs	

- **Task 2:**

We hold these truths to be self-evident, that all men are created equal, that they are endowed by their Creator with certain unalienable rights, that among these are Life, Liberty and the pursuit of Happiness.
From the Declaration of Independence of the United States of America (1776)

Using the information in this pack, and your own knowledge, answer the following question:
To what extend did the US Government's treatment of the Indians meet the ideals expressed in the quotation above?
Explain your answer using appropriate examples.

investigation 13.2 How do Indians live today?

Between 1850 and 1900 the Indians were seen as a vanishing race who would eventually either adopt the White mans' lifestyle – or die. Today they have done neither. There are now more than 2.5 million Indians, over half of whom live off the reservations. They are now rebuilding their tribal traditions and distancing themselves from dependency on US Government support. Today, many aspects of traditional decision-making and leadership (for example the Councils of Elders) are being restored.

The diagrams below and on the next page show some of the ways in which the Indians of today are rebuilding their traditional lifestyles.

Old traditions

- Navaho ceremonies remain central to their spiritual and medical beliefs.
- The tribal council of the 200,000 Navaho Indians still holds meetings in the Navaho language.
- Traditional Navaho metalwork (especially jewellery) brings in much income when sold to tourists.
- Reservation schools teach lessons in English and in the native language.
- In 1993 90 per cent of Indians attended one or more of the 1,000 powwows held in the United States. These are important social events and help to keep alive many traditional dances.

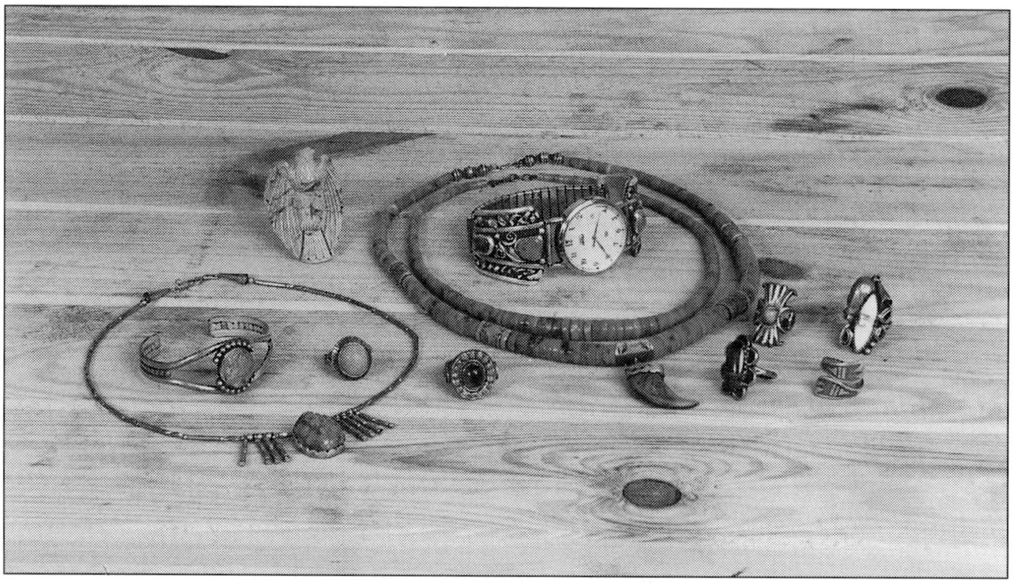

▲ *A photo showing examples of modern jewellery made by Indians in the south-western states*

New developments

Much Indian land in New Mexico lies above uranium deposits providing valuable mineral rights.

Events like protests at Wounded Knee in 1973 (at which two people died) have drawn attention to Indian problems.

A 1988 Act of Congress gave Indians all rights over their own lands.

New organisations like the Native American Rights Fund have won a number of cases winning compensations for broken treaties. The Sioux were awarded $105 million and tribes in Maine won $40 million.

Indians have now opened gambling casinos in 33 states across America. These help to pay for housing.

Since the 1960s the Government has funded education programmes allowing almost all reservation children to attend schools.

things **to do**

- **Task 1:**
  Using the information provided in this investigation, and your own knowledge, answer the following question:
  In what ways have Indians today managed to maintain their traditional values *and* make a place for themselves in modern American society?

Revision questions

THE GREAT PLAINS

1 What were the geographical boundaries of the Great Plains?
2 What was the scenery of the Plains like?
3 What plants grew on the Plains?
4 What animals lived on the Plains?
5 What was the climate of the Plains like?

THE LIFE AND CULTURE OF THE PLAINS INDIANS

1 How did the Indians use horses?
2 Explain the importance of the buffalo to the Indians.
3 Give five uses of the buffalo.
4 Why were the Indians nomadic?
5 Explain how the tepee was perfectly suited to the Indian lifestyle.
6 Why were the Indians polygamous (having more than one wife)?
7 What was exposure and why was it done?
8 How did Indians explain scalping?
9 Give three examples of the 'circles' which influenced Indian religion.
10 Describe the Indian attitude towards the land.

THE FIRST WHITE SETTLERS ON THE PLAINS

1 Why did many people move to Texas from the late 1830s onwards?
2 Why were people encouraged to move to California in 1849 and Colorado and Nevada in the 1860s?
3 What dangers did the early pioneers face on their journey?
4 Explain the concept of 'Manifest Destiny'.
5 What are 'push' and 'pull' factors?
6 Give three examples of 'push' factors and three examples of 'pull' factors which help explain White setlement of the Plains.

THE MORMONS

1 Who founded the Mormon church?
2 Who were Mormon and Moroni?
3 What was the story on the gold plates which became the Book of Mormon?
4 Why were the Mormons so unpopular wherever they settled?
5 Who took over the Church after the founder was murdered?
6 Where did the Mormons decide to move to and why?
7 How was the journey west organised?
8 What advantages and disadvantages did their new home offer?
9 How was their new city designed?
10 What happened in 1858 to disrupt Mormon plans?
11 What happened at Mountain Meadow?
12 Why did the US Government decide to send a new governor to the Mormons in 1857?
13 What agreement was finally made between the Government and the Mormons?

THE COWBOYS AND CATTLE RANCHING

1 Where were the first cowboys from?
2 Why was the Texas 'longhorn' so well suited to the Plains?
3 How did the American Civil War affect the development of cattle ranching?
4 Who was Charles Goodnight?
5 Where did he decide to sell his cattle and how did he intend to get them there?
6 What were the main dangers on the cattle drives?
7 What were 'cow-towns'?
8 Where was the first 'cow-town' and who set it up?
9 Why is John Iliff important?
10 How did the cowboys use a bandana?
11 What were 'chaps' and what were they used for?
12 What did cowboys do in winter?

13 What was the round-up?
14 How did cowboys deal with a stampede?
15 What was the 'beef bonanza'?
16 Give three reasons why the 'beef bonanza' ended.
17 What new inventions speeded up the end of the open range?

HOMESTEADERS – FARMING THE GREAT PLAINS

1 What were homesteaders?
2 What did the Homestead Act of 1862 do to help homesteaders?
3 How did railroads help homesteaders and why?
4 How did newspapers encourage settlers onto the Plains?
5 What were most early homesteads made of?
6 What were the advantages and disadvantages of these buildings?
7 What was used for fuel and why?
8 What problems did women face living on the Plains?
9 What was a 'sodbuster'?
10 Why was it so difficult to fence land and what invention helped to overcome this problem?
11 When was the grasshopper plague?
12 Which Act helped to solve the problem of wood on the Plains and how?
13 Explain the term 'dry-farming'.
14 What other developments improved conditions on the Plains?
15 Where did cowboys and homesteaders come into conflict in the 1890s?
16 How did this conflict end?

GOVERNMENT, LAW AND ORDER

1 What was the difference between a state and a territory?
2 When could a territory apply to become a state?
3 What was 'claim jumping'?
4 Give four reasons to explain why were mining camps so prone to law breaking?
5 What were Miners' Courts?
6 In what ways were Miners' Courts of only limited benefit?
7 What did vigilantes do?
8 Why were vigilantes often as much of a problem as the outlaws?
9 What was the difference between a Federal Marshal and a County Sheriff?

THE FATE OF THE PLAINS INDIANS

1 What 'White man's diseases' helped to wipe out many Indian tribes?
2 What was the Permanent Frontier and why was it set up?
3 When and what was the Trail of Tears?
4 Why did the policy of Separation end by 1851?
5 What was agreed at Fort Laramie in 1851?
6 Why did the policy of Concentration fail so soon after it was set up?
7 Why did the Cheyenne and Arapaho go on the 'warpath' in 1861?
8 Why do the Indians refer to Sand Creek as a massacre?
9 Why did many Indians dislike the steam trains?
10 What new pressures were there on Indian land by the late 1860s?
11 Why did some Whites oppose the idea of extermination of the Indians?
12 What was agreed at Medicine Lodge Creek in 1867?
13 What was Red Cloud's War?
14 What was given to the Sioux in 1868?
15 Why were the Black Hills so important to the Indians?
16 Why did Whites want the Black Hills after 1874?
17 How did the Government propose to get the Black Hills and how did the Indians react to the idea?
18 Describe the plan to destroy the bands of Sitting Bull and Crazy Horse.
19 What did Custer do when he found the Indians?
20 Give five reasons to explain why Custer was defeated.
21 Why is the battle often said to be a 'victory in defeat' for the Indians?
22 What was the Ghost Dance?
23 Why was the Government so afraid of the Ghost Dance?
24 What happened at Wounded Knee Creek in 1890?
25 Why were the Indians so reluctant to live on reservations?
26 What complaints did Indians have about their treatment on reservations?

The American West timeline

Date		What happened
1800:		
1820:		
	1823	Joseph Smith claimed that he was visited by angel called Moroni. Beginnings of the Mormon church.
	1830	*The Book of Mormon* published.
	1834	Permanent Frontier set up – policy of separation began.
	1837	Joseph Smith's bank collapsed and the Mormons fled to Missouri.
1840:		
	1844	Joseph Smith and his brother killed. Brigham Young took over leadership of the church.
	1846–7	Mormons settled at the Great Salt Lake.
	1848	War with Mexico gave the US much land in the south-west – including the Great Salt Lake.
	1849	The California Gold Rush began.
	1851	Fort Laramie agreement – policy of concentration began.
1860:		
	1861	The beginning of the American Civil War.
	1862	Homestead Act allowed settlers 160 acres of free land if they lived and worked on the land for 5 years.
	1864	The Sand Creek Massacre.
	1865	The end of the American Civil War.
	1867	Joseph McCoy set up the first cow town at Abilene, Kansas.
	1868	Fort Laramie Treaty – policy of reservation began.
	1869	A railroad was completed, allowing travel from the east coast to the west.
	1871–2	219,000 claims for land made in Kansas.
	1873	Timber and Culture Act allowed settlers an extra 160 acres if they agreed to plant trees on some of the land.
	1876	The Battle of the Little Bighorn.
	1877	Brigham Young died. The Desert Land Act allowed settlers to buy 640 acres where rainfall was low.
1880:		
	1880s	Period of the Beef Bonanza – the Plains were flooded with cattle and demand began to drop.
	1885–7	43,000 claims for land made in Kansas.
	1886–7	Harsh winter storms and freezing weather on the Plains killed huge numbers of cattle.
	1890	The Mormon church gave up polygamy. Battle of Wounded Knee ended Indian Wars.
1900		